POTS *and* PEOPLE

that have shaped the heritage of medieval and later England

by

Maureen Mellor

ASHMOLEAN MUSEUM, OXFORD
1997

ASHMOLEAN MUSEUM PUBLICATIONS

ARCHAEOLOGY, HISTORY AND CLASSICAL STUDIES

To the Durham family

The Ashmolean Museum is grateful to The Greening Lamborn Trust
and the W. A. Pantin Charitable Trust for grants towards the publica-
tion of this book..

ISBN 1 85444 080 2

Abbreviations
OAHS Oxford Architectural and Historical Society
OUAS Oxford University Archaeological Society

Designed and typeset in Bembo by Andrew Ivett
Printed and bound in Great Britain by Clifford Press Ltd, Coventry

Contents

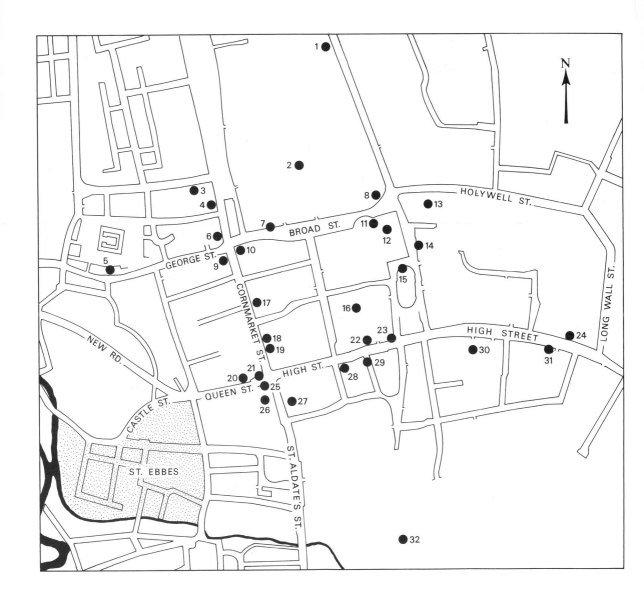

Fig. 1. This plan of the City and University of Oxford is based on Alden's map of 1897 as used by Percy Manning. Substantial changes have occurred, particularly in the St. Ebbe's area. Sites referred to in the text (pre-1940) are as follows: 1. Forestry Laboratory (St. John's College); 2. Trinity College (Durham Hall); 3. Randolph Hotel; 4. Oxenford Hall (19-21 Magdalen Street); 5. New Corn Exchange, George Street; 6. 3 Magdalen Street; 7. Balliol College; 8. New Bodleian Library; 9. Leopold Arms (The Bocardo Gaol, 36 Cornmarket Street); 10. Broad/Cornmarket Street; 11. Bodleian Tunnel; 12. Clarendon Building Enclosure; 13. Hertford College City Ditch; 14. Hertford College; 15. Radcliffe Camera/Square; 16. Lincoln Hall; 17. 18-20 Cornmarket; 18. 7 Cornmarket (Civet Cat); 19. 3 Cornmarket Street; 20. Three Cups Inn (Queen Street); 21. Carfax Church; 22. Brasenose (Quatercentenary building); 23. Brasenose (St. Mary's Entry); 24. Masonic Hall (50A High Street); 25. Glyn Mills Bank, Carfax; 26. Fleur-de-Luce (117-119 St Aldates - Battes Inn); 27. Town Hall, City Buildings; 28. London and County Bank (Stodley Inn); 29. King Edward Street; 30. University College; 31. New Examination Schools (Old Angel Inn); 32. Meadow Building, Christ Church.

Fig. 2. The Medieval Room with Rhenish stoneware seltzers and drinking jugs in the foreground. Eighteenth-nineteenth century.

Introduction

The pottery in the medieval room of the Ashmolean Museum has a remarkable story to tell (Fig. 2). The material is not old by the standards of many of the Museum's collections, but it is important nationally as a rich resource of complete vessels, dating to the medieval and later periods, whose provenance can be linked with the historical and topographical evidence to give a broader picture. This reflects the lives of the scholarly consumer within the University, the merchants and inhabitants of the commercial centre and the townsmen living in the suburbs. It illustrates the development of an ancient craft which has been studied perhaps more closely than any other, and it also illustrates the zeal and enthusiasm of a number of Oxford's amateur archaeologists. The vessels on display are only the tip of an iceberg of material in the reserve collection, where there are many vessels which add breadth to the present account, and are referred to where appropriate.

Our tour of the display will start with the broad groups of ceramic in the collection, followed by an account of their methods of manufacture. We see how ceramic technology was advanced by distin-

guished pioneer scientists working in the seventeenth-century Oxford, while two others, men with Oxford connections, were advancing the manufacturing process. We then turn to the major stylistic and technological innovations which provide an historic framework, and thereby an independant chronology. What we learn from these developing patterns must reflect on the economic, social, cultural and political history of this part of England, and some of the conclusions are set out.

The second part of the volume concentrates on the fount of the collection: the men without whose energy, vision and appreciation Oxford pottery studies would have remained at a very rudimentary level. We chart the early life of Arthur Evans, an undergraduate of the Victorian period who was later honoured for his excavations of a great Mediterranean civilization. Two more Victorian undergraduates, Thomas Jackson and Percy Manning, had totally contrasting academic lives, while a fourth, an Edwardian undergraduate, was drawn to the Ashmolean through his passion for pottery and played a major role in the formation of the later medieval collection. Of the four, Jackson died after an illness at the beginning of the Great War, while Evans was president of three of

5

Fig. 3. Hand-made coarse wares; earthenware from local production centres. Eleventh-twelfth century.

the most distinguished academic societies in the country. The remaining two both saw active service, the older man, Manning, died, the younger, Lawrence, became eulogised by a world looking for a hero in the face of unbelievable devastation, an accolade which he carried with increasing difficulty while continuing his interest in Oxford's past.

After the Great War, another undergraduate was to emerge during the depression years of the 1930s, a larger-than-life personality who went on to inspire a generation of younger scholars. He and other scholars fill out the story of the Ashmolean's collection. The fruits of their gifted, inquiring minds kept Oxford ceramics in the forefront of research in Britain and Europe. Since the Second World War the focus has turned more to the intrinsic qualities of individual pot sherds, so that increasingly it became possible to make a more confident historical story from assemblages of associated fragments rather than complete vessels. Interestingly this followed a trend, replicated in other cities in Britain, but not fully explained, for the Museum's collections to access more fragments and fewer complete vessels. The story told by the newer collections is more assertive but less visual: the Ashmolean's collection is exceptional because it is comprised chiefly of complete vessels, a monument to late nineteenth and early twentieth century achievement and one of the most important resources of material culture in England.

Medieval and later ceramics are found on archaeological sites all over Europe. Ceramic archaeological studies have traditionally been the preserve of historians and archaeologists, but increasingly archaeological results are being digested by the Art World, as well as by contemporary craftsmen. The study of ceramics is a key archaeological activity and this brief guide to the collection curated by the Ashmolean's Antiquities Department aims to bring this material within reach of a wider audience, so enabling a greater enjoyment and understanding of the past.

Part I:
The Ceramic Groups in the Collection

Three groups of ceramic occur in the archaeological record, earthenware, stoneware and porcelain. Each vessel can also be placed into one of two classes: coarse wares and finewares; coarse wares are generally associated with use in the kitchen, for cooking, storage and preparing of food or industrial processes (Fig. 3) while finewares are often decorated and may be used for serving or be merely for display (Fig. 4).

Earthenware Types in the Collection

The first ceramic type and the most common in archaeological excavations and in the collection is earthenware. Earthenware is the lowest fired of all

Fig. 4. Wheel-thrown finewares; earthenware from the Brill/Boarstall workshops in central Buckinghamshire. Fourteenth-fifteenth century.

(700–1200 C), made from secondary clays which contain a wide variety of decomposed impurities which, when fired, give a range of colours – an oxidising atmosphere gives a variety of hues of reds and browns, while a reducing atmosphere gives greys and blacks.

This type of clay with its small particle size is easier to work for the potter. Earthenware is porous and needs a glaze to make it water tight. The Oxford region had abundant supplies of such clay, all of which were exploited for making bricks, tiles and pottery. A cartload of clay would make some 2,000 pots.

Earthenware clay was favoured by medieval craftsmen and artisans at the Brill/Boarstall workshops, ten miles to the east of Oxford, for an astonishing variety of jugs and other utilitarian pots, such as cook pots, storage jars and bowls (Figs. 4, 31 and 32).

In the medieval period the lord of the manor at Brill required the potter to pay a license fee to dig clay, and it was this raw material on which he, the lord, made his profit. The potter was a consumer of clay. A reeve's account of 1279 gives 4s. 6d. for 'clay-gavel', and clay gavel was entered regularly in the steward's accounts in the thirteenth and fourteenth centuries.

The oral evidence collected in 1906 at the Leafield pottery in north-west Oxfordshire, highlighted how three generations of the Franklin family in the nineteenth century had exploited different lenses of the same clay deposit; one lens was used for finer earthenware pottery, the lower beds for brick and drain-pipes.

Unglazed earthenware is historically more common than glazed, but the plain functional coarse wares are not very well represented in the Ashmolean collection, in comparison with the elegant decorated and lead-glazed finewares. This may be because vessels used in cooking have a higher rate of breakage than those vessels used for decanting liquids, rather than a bias in collecting. Vessels imported from beyond the Oxford region, using earthenware clay, include estuarine clays of the Stamford area in south Lincolnshire, pottery from the coal measure seams centred on the Midlands, and the Reading Beds of the London area (see Figs. 25, 29 and 47).

Earthenware products were made locally and supplied the urban and rural population until the seventeenth century, when other ceramic groups became available.

Another earthenware, tin-glazed earthenware, is made from primary clay which is less plastic and less easily worked than the iron rich earthenware, and it

Fig. 5. **Wheel-thrown tin-glaze earthenware pharmaceutical pots, made in London or Holland. Seventeenth-eighteenth century.**

fires to a white colour. Introduced to Spain by medieval Islamic potters, tin-glaze technology then spread to Italy and was initially imported to England from Italy in the form of containers for treacle, exotic fruits etc. Later, smaller containers with opaque and white glaze for ointments, herbal remedies or drugs, were made in the Low Countries, used by apothecaries and 'comfittmakers'. These sources were centred on the towns of Antwerp, and later Amsterdam, Haarlem, Utrecht and Delft in north Holland. Immigrant potters moved to England from Antwerp, to escape religious persecution, and set up in Norwich and London.

Seventeenth-century pharmaceutical pots, plain or polychrome, form a significant part of the tin-glazed products in the collection, which come from the University and commercial areas. Drugs and other preparations manufactured and sold by apothecaries were stored and dispensed from jars, some large with straight sides for dry products, others spherical on a trumpet-shaped foot with handle and spout for liquids. Both have wide mouths under which string could be tied to hold down parchment covers. Ointment pots were used for dispensing medicines prepared in semi-liquid or paste form (Fig. 5).

These large pharmaceutical pots are comparatively rare amongst the excavated assemblages of the Oxford's south western quarter of St. Ebbe's (Figs. 1 and 91). The most frequent tin-glazed product from these

7

Fig. 6. Moulded polychrome flatware and wheel-thrown hollow wares in tin-glaze earthenware probably made in London. Second half seventeenth and mid seventeenth century respectively.

suburbs were chamber pots, dating to the eighteenth century, but few of these feature in the collection.

Open flatwares, often decorated with highly coloured metal oxides, in the most fashionable style would have been used for display or as tablewares, evidence that a new etiquette was evolving amongst the inhabitants of Oxford. Other new tableware innovations included the globular and cylindrical mugs copying pewter and silver shapes. Such pots are often described in inventories as 'marbled' (Fig. 6).

Tin-glaze earthenware was expensive compared with the locally produced earthenwares. The majority of the tin-glaze earthenwares excavated from Oxford in the collection were supplied by the London production centres, Lambeth and Southwark or made in Holland. A few vessels only are attributed to Italy.

Gallipots, usually known as albarellos, cylindrical or semi-cylindrical earthenware pots of various sizes, begin to be listed locally in probate inventories as early as 1612, but at this date these may still have been continental in origin, although tin-glaze earthenwares were made in England as early as the third quarter of the sixteenth century.

WILLIAM CLARKE'S INVENTORY DATED 1612

4 galy pots and 3 glasses	6d.
For black potts and gally pots	3s. 6d.
13 stone potts	3s. 0d.

1 dyzen of suckinge bottles	8d.
For stone potts	3s. 6d.
5 dyzen of glasses	4s. 0d.
Yellow round plate and candlestick	18d.

The inventory shows that a range of glassware for drinking and desserts was becoming popular along with 'galy pots' made in tin-glaze earthenware and 'stone-pots' made in the Rhineland. Yellow glazed wares from either the Surrey/Hampshire border or possibly from Staffordshire were also in use in Oxford at the end of Elizabeth I's reign.

Bowls, plates and dishes associated with the table are also poorly represented in the collection. There is no evidence of local tin-glaze earthenware manufacture, but they were imported to the region in increasing quantities from the early seventeenth until the mid eighteenth century. Further examples of English tin-glaze (delftware) may be seen in the Robert Hall Warren Collection, and the important collection of Italian maiolica is available in the Fortnum Room in the galleries of the Department of Western Art.

Stoneware Types in the Collection

The second ceramic group is stoneware. Stoneware clay is also a secondary clay, but with a fusible mineral that allowed it to withstand very high firing temperatures (1200-1300 C) and it was consequently more durable than earthenware. It was particularly favoured for 'vessels for retaining the penetrating salts and spirits of the chymists'. The early vessels may have been luxury goods in colleges and private dwellings but by the early seventeenth century were more popular in taverns and communal eating houses in the commercial centre than in the ordinary households of the suburbs.

The high-fired stoneware, which had been developed and made in the Rhineland and western Belgium from the thirteenth century, was much better suited to use and less liable to break than contemporary earthenwares.

Salt-glazed stonewares were shipped in large quantities to this country from the Rhineland after the Renaissance in northern Europe, often as ballast in the bottom of Dutch ships, trading to the east coast of England and sold at competitive prices (Fig. 7). It was also later shipped to the colonies in America and Australia. The major production centres were in Germany, at Frechen and Cologne, at Siegburg and Westerwald and further west at Langerwehe and Raeren.

Fig. 7. **Wheel-thrown stoneware drinking vessels made in the Rhineland, Germany; a late sixteenth century inventory in Oxford records 'great' stone pots costing 4*d*. and smaller ones at 2*d*. They range in size from a 'fist' to 'large bellied vessels'. Sixteenth century.**

Many of the earlier stonewares imported to this country did not travel far inland, and the paucity of evidence in the Ashmolean collections is typical: Siegburg and Langerwehe drinking wares are rare from local archaeological deposits. Only three Raeren-type funnel-necked jugs (see Fig. 7 top left) and half a dozen grey glazed Raeren mugs of the later fifteenth–mid sixteenth century are present (see Fig. 7, foreground). Cologne-type squat mugs with sprigged oak-leaf and rose decoration are absent from the collection and only one dated *Schnelle* from Siegburg was recovered from the Old Angel Inn (see Fig. 43). Some dozen examples of the Frechen/Cologne *Bartmann* jugs of the mid–late sixteenth century with portrait medallions are present (Fig. 7). Thereafter, a steady flow of the plain straight-necked Frechen jugs with their globular body and *Bartmann* jugs with armorial devices, both real and fake, gain a monopoly, until the end of the seventeenth century (Figs. 48 and 71). These are replaced by the colourful Westerwald jugs and cylindrical tankards with royal ciphers (see Figs. 50 and 51). The commercial success of the stoneware trade stimulated several attempts to manufacture the ware in Britain.

Dr Robert Plot, the first custodian of the Ashmolean Museum (1640-96), wrote the first-ever survey of the county, *Natural History of Oxford-shire* (1677), in which he praises the special properties of some local clay, which may have properties similar to stoneware clays. He writes:

'At Marsh Baldon Heath, and Nuneham Courtney (to the south of Oxford) they have a sort of Earth of ductile parts which put in the fire scarcely cracks, and has been formerly used by *Potters* but upon what account I know not, now neglected'. Again in south-east Oxfordshire, 'About Nettlebed they make a sort of brick so very strong that whereas at most places they are unloaded by hand, I have seen these shot out of the cart after the manner of stones to mend the Highways and yet none of them broken; but this I suppose must rather be ascribed to the nature of the clay, than to the skill of the Artificers in making and burning'. By the nineteenth century Nettlebed was

Fig. 8. Wheel-thrown stoneware 'ale-mugs' made in London, inscribed with college, inn or personal names. Two tankards were stamped with metal dyes: a plant impression (8a, second shelf, left) and an oriental pheasant (8b, second shelf right); the plant impression is similar to the brass seal matrixes used by Dwight. These are believed to be cut by the Dutch Medalist, Arondeux (1655–*c*.1727). Late Seventeenth-eighteenth century.

a

b

advertising 'The Finest Clay for Stoneware in South of England'. Taken together with Plot's observations, it was clear that the clay was capable of being fired to a high temperature.

English salt-glazed stonewares had largely replaced the Rhenish stonewares locally by the early eighteenth century. The majority of London stonewares in the collections, are the cylindrical tankards or 'ale-mugs' dated to the second quarter of the eighteenth century and occur in three sizes: half pint, pint and quart (Fig. 8). The 'ale-mugs' in the collection are mainly from sites which were colleges, taverns and coaching inns. College mugs included a half pint mug inscribed 'Wad Coll' found in student lodgings opposite Wadham College. Stoneware tankards were often incised with the name of the licensee, and sprig moulded panels, depicting the Inn sign were added. Ale houses represented include the Weirs Inn *c.*1757 with a medallion of three salmon, inscribed 'White Weyers', which was dredged out of the Thames opposite Christ Church Meadow (see also Fig. 68); Charles Field, licensee of the Red Lion in the High Street, had his name inscribed on mugs and one vessel was dated 1762. The lion was a symbol of nobility and courage and the red lion originally signi-fied allegiance to John of Gaunt. A fragment of a medallion from the Bear Inn was retrieved from George Street (Fig. 8 in the foreground). The Bear (1432-1801) with its premises on the corner of Alfred Street and the High Street was one of the largest taverns in Oxford and later became a coaching inn. The bear and ragged staff were emblems of Richard Neville, Earl of Warwick and the chained bear was identified with the sport of bear baiting. Another coaching inn, the Old Angel Inn, also identified their ale mugs, several examples identified the King family as licensees with a variety of sprig-moulded angels (Fig. 68). The angel was a religious sign, a symbol of salutation.

The name James Knight was incised on a half pint mug found on the tenement adjoining The George on the corner of Magdalen and George Street (Fig. 8 top right).

It was the practise to send customers home with a full mug, the mug to be returned the following day, but the provenance of many of these marked tankards show how they were often discarded well away from the premises from which they originated, perhaps after a night of revelry! It was clearly in the interest of the licensees to be able to identify their pots.

Fig. 9. Moulded stoneware Loving Cups inscribed 'William and Mary Smith, Farndon 1793' and [Eliza]beth Townend June 7th 1760. Made in Nottingham. Eighteenth century. Unprovenanced 1938.239 and 238. (Ht. 22.5 cm.; 24 cm.).

Bottles imitating the Rhenish vessels, pitchers, storage jars such as pickling pots or snuff jars are not well represented, but globular mugs, imitating metal shapes, are more frequent in the collection (see top left Fig. 8).

A few specimens of English stoneware from Staffordshire, Nottinghamshire and Derbyshire, first manufactured about 1690, were recovered from the excavations. Excavated vessels from these north Midlands production centres are however rare in the city (Fig. 66).

The commemorative wares, such as loving cups display considerable technical and artistic merit, the high content of mica in the iron slip gives an iridescent finish to these vessels (Fig. 9). Those in the collection however are not from local archaeological deposits. A third vessel in the reserve collection is inscribed 'Mary Sims June 24th Anno Dom. 1724'. Nineteenth-century Derbyshire production centres specialised in a wide range of bottles including containers for 'blacking' used for cleaning the cast iron fireplaces. Hearth and ink bottles are not surprisingly well represented. Mineral water, in particular from the Rhineland became fashionable during the eighteenth and nineteenth centuries and was sold in distinctive stoneware bottles (Fig. 10). A nineteenth century trade card shows the

Fig. 11. Moulded red earthenware Jackfield-type teapot with black glaze, made either in the north Midlands or London. Eighteenth century. Brasenose 1886.577. (Ht. 6.5 cm.).

demand for mineral and aerated water and advertised eleven different varieties including 'Genuine German seltzer water' as well as English ginger beer.

White earthenwares had been very popular in the seventeenth century and stoneware potters were keen to emulate this fashion. Staffordshire white dipped salt-glazed stoneware, developed c.1710 is however barely represented amongst the collections nor from more recent excavations in Oxford.

The true fine white salt-glaze stoneware was first developed in this country by John Dwight at his Fulham workshops in London (see Portrait of Dwight in Methods of Manufacture later). These were copied, manufactured and successfully marketed in Staffordshire in the 1720s. Shapes included teawares, influenced by early porcelain and contemporary silver shapes and included a small fragmentary teacup with enamelled decoration recorded in 1906 from the Leopold Arms 'as the first specimen of this class yet found in Oxford' (for shape of cup from the same provenance see Fig. 89). Salt-glazed stoneware dinner services are absent from the collection but have been excavated in the south western suburbs of Oxford. This material is now held by the Oxfordshire Museums Service but Sir Arthur Church's English salt-glaze collection can be seen in the Department of Western Art galleries.

A white clay source was cited by Plot at Shotover, a mile to the east of the City and was used during the Civil War for making tobacco-pipes. A reference to this same white clay occurs in a letter of 1759, written to the director of the Sèvres Factory in France, implying that it was used to manufacture 'China'

Fig. 10. Moulded stoneware mineral water containers, made in the Rhineland, two with stamped marks, the third with 'P' in cobalt blue, possibly a batch mark. Eighteenth and nineteenth century.

locally (see Portrait of Brolliet in Methods of Manufacture later).

Red stoneware was developed by Dutch potters in the late seventeenth century in London and later in Staffordshire. The Staffordshire red clay was thrown and turned to a fine-walled section; burnished and sprig moulded decoration from engraved brass or copper moulds was then added. Only one red stoneware vessel is in the collection from local excavations: a genuine Elers teapot from Jackson's Collection at the Radcliffe Camera. Only two other teapots are known from excavations, one in London and another from Temple Balsall in the West Midlands. The black glossy glazed earthenwares were manufactured in Shropshire and Staffordshire during the eighteenth century, the repertoire including teapots (Fig. 11), globular drinking mugs and chamber pots. Black Basalt, a distinctive dry-bodied black stoneware, was manufactured in Staffordshire after 1750 and a few examples from archaeological deposits are in the collection.

Porcelain Types in the Collection

The third group of ceramic, porcelain, is made from a primary clay (see also the Marshall Collection of Worcester Porcelain). This is the highest firing of all the clay types, to between 1200-1450 C, when it becomes translucent. Chinese porcelain vessels were imported to Holland by Portugese traders; and from the early seventeenth century onwards they became very popular in the Low Countries and greatly influenced the indigeneous tin-glaze earthenware potters. Imported China ware was keenly sought after at this time by the well-to-do: it was used by ladies at home and in the commercial tea houses and it remained expensive throughout the seventeenth and early eighteenth centuries. By the nineteenth century several specialist tea-dealers were operating in the market towns of Oxfordshire: Bampton, Banbury and Witney amongst others, indicating that tea was available to a much wider population than previously and at least one warehouse is known in Oxford (Fig. 13).

In the 1660s the word 'china' was first used to include all the plates, bowls, saucers, jars and dishes imported from the Orient.

The earliest porcelain made in Europe was possibly the Medici porcelain ewer of *c.*1580, manufactured at the experimental factory in Florence (the ewer is displayed in the Fortnum Room in the Department of Western Art). The first Oxford Collection of Chinese porcelain was rescued by A. B.

Fig. 12. Wheel-thrown Chinese blue and white porcelain cup, ornamented peach in the interior, blue wavy design and landscape on the exterior, marked on the bottom within blue circle, 'made in the reign of Shing Fa of the Great Ming' (dynasty). The stamp is an archaizing one commonly used in the eighteenth century to which this piece belongs. Emden Collection. Radcliffe Camera 1911.261. (Ht. 6 cm.).

13

Emden, the eminent medieval historian, from the Radcliffe Camera in the University area in 1911 (see Part II and Fig. 12).

Despite early English experiments with soft-paste porcelain (see Portrait of Dwight in Methods of Manufacture later) there is no evidence that they were marketed successfully, and the secret of soft-paste porcelain is usually accredited to Saint Cloud in France, while hard-paste porcelain was invented by two Germans from Dresden in 1708. The factory moved to Meissen two years later, where royal patronage gave it a competitive edge over English potteries, which depended on commercial success. English porcelain was an expensive commodity when compared with Oriental porcelain.

The English factories were set up in 1740s. Isolated mid eighteenth-century examples of English soft paste porcelain tea bowls and cups have been collected from the University area, still made in the traditional Chinese form with no handles. By the end of the eighteenth century a heavy tax on silver persuaded many people to buy the less expensive porcelain, and the British potteries expanded to meet this

Fig. 13. A retail card advertising Wise's Foreign China Warehouse, selling chinese porcelain jars, tea cups and saucers, in St. Clement's Oxford. Such depositories were often places of assignation! Nineteenth century. Courtesy of Bodleian Library.

demand. Hard paste porcelains replaced the soft-fired vessels in the early-mid nineteenth century.

These three broad groups of ceramic in the collection: earthenware, stoneware and porcelain each provided a range of vessels varying in quality and style yet each found a substantial market. Each group of ceramic lends itself to different methods of manufacture.

Methods of Manufacture

The complete or near-complete pots in the collection illustrate many aspects of manufacture and technology.

Plot in his survey, *Natural History of Oxford-shire*, sets out (amongst other topics) the topography and the availability of the essential prerequisites of pottery and the tile making — clay, water and wood — in the seventeenth century countryside. He was interested in people and their achievements, and was intrigued by '*Arts* that concern the *Formation of Earth*', such as clays and their hidden potential. He wrote: 'So that, that which hath lain buryed and useless to the *Owners*, may become beneficial to them by reason of this manufacture, and many working hands get good livelyhoods, not to speak of the very considerable sums of *English Coyn* annually kept at home by it.' This sentiment was to be echoed later by nineteenth-century philanthropists.

Initially earthenware pottery making in most parts of the country was probably seasonal, an occupation combined on occasions with agriculture. The clay was dug by hand in late autumn, the frost and rain broke it up and made it easier to work; a tradition passed down since medieval times, but still practised at Leafield in north west Oxfordshire during the nineteenth century. In late Spring, the potters resumed their craft.

London tin-glaze potters mixed their own clay: ordinary clay was obtained locally but the vital calcareous clay had to be imported, initially from East Anglia via the port of Great Yarmouth, and brought by water to London. Later a suitable clay was found in nearby Kent.

The London stoneware industry based at the Fulham Pottery used white clay from Dorset, mixing it with sand imported from the Isle of Wight. Both the tin-glaze earthenware potters and their contemporaries specialising in stoneware worked throughout the year, engaged in the processes of manufacture.

Making of the Pots

Pots could be made either by hand or thrown on a wheel. Some potters working with earthenware clays used both techniques depending on the size and shape of the vessel. Others preferred to make all their products by hand, even though the more advanced technology of wheel throwing was available in the region. Some clays, particularly those with small particles of flint, lent themselves to hand building techniques better — coil made pots continued to be made and used in the county until the fifteenth century. Elsewhere in the region potters using sand tempered clays threw all their vessels on a fast wheel as early as the second quarter of the thirteenth century, as at the Brill/Boarstall workshops.

Tin-glaze earthenwares were usually thrown on a wheel, but some flatwares were formed by pressing a clay slab into moulds (press-moulding). The majority of the stonewares were wheel thrown as were the delicate porcelain teawares from China. European porcelain clays were less easy to work with, so press-moulding and slip casting methods were employed more readily.

Glazing and Decoration

Glazing made the pots less porous. Initially the earthenwares were dusted with a lead galena, later brushed with a water suspension as at the workshops of the Brill/Boarstall potters. It was not until the later fourteenth century that pots were dipped into glaze at those workshops. Metal oxides such as copper filings were added to give a rich green or mottled green colour. A variety of slips and other decorative methods further enhanced the medieval jugs and pitchers (see Figs. 32 and 77).

The industrious Plot recorded and published his observations of another county in his *Natural History of the County of Stafford-shire* (1686). Clearly impressed by the North Staffordshire potters, he describes the techniques of making decorated lead-glazed slipwares in coloured liquid clays, mottled wares and the use of powdered lead ore. Jackson's collection from the Radcliffe Camera (see Part II) included the only known example from Oxford of a casserole and a milk pail in Staffordshire mottled brown ware; a cylindrical tankard with an 'AR' excise mark is one of only half a dozen from the city. Moulded Staffordshire or Bristol slipware dishes and drinking vessels are found in small quantities on most sites dating to the late seventeenth–early eighteenth century (Fig. 14).

Fig. 14. Moulded and wheel-thrown slipwares and mottled wares from the Staffordshire Potteries, including an unusual milk pail. Dr. Plot was very enamoured with the slipware technique. Eighteenth century. Jackson Collection.

In 1906 Manning, a local antiquarian (see Part II) found that the Leafield Crown Pottery in the heart of Wychwood Forest in north west Oxfordshire had returned to brush application - 'brown ores' described as lead dioxide and later red lead were favoured. Both fired to an orange or rich brown glaze (see Fig. 53). The method of glazing earthenware probably varied from one production centre to another.

White tin oxide, an expensive commodity purchased as a powder, was suspended in a lead glaze and fired to a creamy white opacity, giving the characteristic covering to tin-glaze earthenwares. On the early decorative flatwares it was often applied on the upper surfaces only while the bases were covered with transparent lead glaze to reduce the cost. A variety of colourants was used for the hand-painted decoration. Lead and tin oxides were both mined in England but copper oxides so popular on medieval jugs and pitchers were imported from abroad.

The sixteenth century Rhenish finewares from Siegburg were unglazed. Later stonewares used lead glaze and then salt-glazing became ubiquitious. This technique probably originated in Germany, where salt mines were such a rich resource in antiquity, and is achieved by common salt being thrown onto the kiln fire rather than being applied directly to the individual pots. The glaze varies from a light glossing of the surface to thick brown mottled texturing (orange-peel or 'tiger skin' see Fig. 48).

Cobalt oxide was later added to the salt glaze, giving a bright blue decoration; manganese oxide, another colouring agent resulted in dark purples. The London stonewares imitated the German decorative techniques: sprig-moulding was employed for the face masks and medallions used on Rhenish *Bartmann* jugs and later English stoneware: for the devices on bottles and the applied inn signs on the 'ale-mugs'. Later the English potters added white or brown slip to their repertoire and lathe-turned decoration was introduced. In Nottingham and Derbyshire, sprig-moulding, free-hand incising, roller stamping and stamped decoration were the favoured techniques.

In porcelain the body and the glaze matures together giving a thick body glaze layer, which does not chip as with the tin-glaze earthenwares. Hand-painted underglaze blue and polychrome decoration, and later overglaze enamels enhanced the pots, first used sparingly and later to mask the entire body. European porcelains initially copied the Chinese decorative techniques but new designs reflecting European tastes then flowered.

Firing

The firing season for smaller local earthenware industries was probably during the summer months. The clay soils support extensive woodland, which was exploited for fuel — a great deal of wood was necessary to sustain just one firing.

Much medieval woodland was owned by the King; historical evidence records that potters were allowed the small branches from the trees in the King's forest of Bernwood in 1255, and at the Royal forest of Wychwood the potters could purchase coppice. Despite this, there were numerous offenders against the 'vert'. Nineteen were recorded from Leafield; among them Richard le Poter and Nicholas le Poter were each fined 12d. for wholesale and persistent taking of the King's wood. Such a fine would have been very severe given that the average daily wage was 1/2d. per day, or possibly less for a working potter. Langley Palace, a royal hunting lodge in Leafield, might nevertheless have acted initially as a commercial focus, a ready consumer for the potter's products. A contemporary parallel may be found at Brill, in Buckinghamshire.

Pottery was made at Brill and in the adjoining parish of Boarstall in central west Buckinghamshire (the latter was within the manor of Brill until 1213 and possibly a century after). Both lay within the royal forest of Bernwood (Fig. 15). In the Hundred Rolls for Brill, there were recorded ten *furna vel plurima at 3d*. each in 1255. Professor Martyn Jope excavated part of the site of four superimposed kilns in the 1950s, where he estimated there were 25,000 pots and the remains of 20,000 pots in a waster dump.

The wood firing of these pots took place in a single or double updraught kiln, with a central pedestal, and the products indicate a well regulated oxidising atmosphere, although wood firing always gives diversity to the end products. The four kilns excavated on an east-facing slope away from the prevailing wind showed considerable variety in the method of construction and quality. Plot records in the seventeenth century that turf, cut out like bricks, was used as domestic fuel in parishes closer to Oxford and turf may also have been adopted by some potters.

Oral evidence collected by Manning in 1906 at Leafield indicates that faggots of thorn and furze from the Forest had been used to fire the kilns, although coal was also used in the eighteenth and nineteenth centuries. Pots and bricks were sometimes fired in the same kilns at Leafield and Brill in the nineteenth century. Manning describes the kiln at Leafield as having five stoke holes, and it may therefore have been rectangular in form.

Similar kilns were in use at Brill, where bricks were fired together with fine hollow wares (earthenware cups) — stacked in fireclay containers (saggers) used to protect the pottery products from direct flames, were fired together in the sixteenth and early seventeenth century. Such multi-flue kilns are not found in the Low Countries. An initial firing with wood completed the drying process and medieval jugs were often placed upside down in the kiln (Fig. 16). At Leafield the fires were banked up with coal and the firing continued, taking two days and one night in all. Control of the kiln temperature during the firing period was essential to prevent shattering of the pots and Alec Franklin stayed up all night tending the kiln.

Fig. 15. A romantic topographical oil painting by Edmund John Niemann, dated 1858: 'At Brill, Bucks, Wootton and Ludgershall in the distance', with ceramic workshops, drying sheds and broken down bottle kiln in the foreground. Courtesy of Buckinghamshire County Museum.

Prior to the introduction of domed kiln structures designed to conserve heat, pots were satisfactorily fired in a clamp or bonfire kiln. Shallow pits or trenches were dug, a bed of combustible material was laid, the pots placed on the top and the fuel lit, more fuel was then added to cover the pots and complete the firing. The choice of fuel was critical for a good result as was the strength of the wind. On occasions, the fire was dampened down by adding green wood or foliage, causing a more controlled cooling down period.

Tin-glaze earthenwares were fired to a biscuit state, then glazed, decorated and finally fired a second time. The use of saggars also ensured a more even temperature and made best use of the space in the kiln. Other kiln furniture included kiln spacers, pegs and trivets used to keep the vessels separate in these saggars, and their marks are often present on the finished article.

Early kilns used for firing tin-glaze earthenwares were rectangular with a stokehole at one end feeding a fire-box extending underneath the main chamber, with flues up the side walls through which the hot gasses circulated into the main chamber, finally passing out of vents in the roof vault. Later kilns were bottle shaped, with five or seven stoke-holes around their base.

Fig. 16. Medieval jugs were often stacked upside down in the kiln. This wheel-thrown earthenware jug with applied red strips and yellow glaze shows tell-tale bleeding of the iron-rich strips. Mid-late thirteenth century. Randolph Hotel 1836.1865 p13. (Ht. 29 cm.).

Dwight's stoneware kilns at Fulham were similar to those used by the contemporary tin-glaze earthenware potters working in London, which in turn copied those common in the Rhineland in Germany. They were described as 'built about eight feet square. Arched at the top like a vault with holes to let out the smoke'; later bottle kilns were adopted. Although wood was used by Dwight, the early eighteenth century saw the widespread adoption of coal.

Bottle kilns used for earthenwares still exist in the region, one at Nettlebed in south east Oxfordshire, another at Winchcombe in Gloucestershire where this century pottery was again made in the English tradition.

Water Resources

Clay and fuel were obvious requirements but water was also necessary to prepare the clay and make the pottery vessels. Rivers, streams and springs could provide this, but on a hilltop site as at Leafield the water from the village pond was distributed by water cart.

Fig. 17. An engraved retail card showing a bottle kiln close to water transport, with pottery packed in 'crates' in the foreground. Nineteenth century. Courtesy of Bodleian Library.

In London, the potters preferred to be close to the river Thames not only for water supply but also to keep down transport costs (Fig. 17).

Pottery was a local craft industry up to the seventeenth century, serving local and regional needs. Potters although skilled were not well regarded in the community and very little is known about the individual potters or indeed any craftsmen or women in the medieval period. Two potters from Brill distinguished themselves and appeared in documents for the first quarter of the thirteenth century — Sampson le Poter and Walter le Poter — and there is also a twelfth-century reference to a Ralph Poter.

It was a precarious craft and would not have attracted those interested in making money. They had no guild to set and enforce standards and were therefore dependent on the lord of the manor or the King's generosity for their clay and fuel, as seen earlier by those named men before the King's bench! Pottery guilds did exist on the Continent in the Low Countries, such as one at Antwerp which was concerned with the interests of the tin-glaze earthenware potters, some of whom later came to England. A separate guild existed for red earthenware potters, whose work was less well regarded, than the tin-glaze earthenware pottery. A similar demarcation was in operation in Catalonia in Spain.

Plot only mentions in passing the potters of the Oxford region in his survey of the county. We must conclude that in the second half of the seventeenth century there were no major pottery industries locally that caught his attention. However, at this period individual potters, men of great ability, began to emerge and were noted in the historical record. Two such men, with local connections, made a considerable contribution to ceramic history: one was to become famous for his English stonewares and experiments with porcelain, the other excelled in industrial espionage, introducing English innovations and technology to France.

— PORTRAIT —

Chemist, Master Potter and Entrepreneur: J Dwight.

Plot's survey gives an invaluable insight and enthusiastic account of John Dwight (c.1633-1703), 'son of a yeoman farmer from North Hinksey near Oxford'. Dwight apparently read 'Civil Law and Physick a little, but mostly Chymistry' at Christ Church, Oxford, although 'there is no evidence that he matriculated' (Fig. 18).

Dwight set up the first English stoneware factory at Fulham in London and was granted a patent in 1672 by Charles II. He successfully manufactured imitations of Rhenish stonewares 'Stone or Cologne wares such as D'Alva Bottles, Jugs, Noggins', D'Alva bottles refer to *Bartmann* jugs, formerly known as Bellarmines or Greybeards. Noggins are straight-sided cylindrical mugs or tankards ('ale-mugs') as well as 'Hessian wares' believed to be crucibles for industrial purposes.

Dwight was encouraged in his venture by Robert Hooke, the scientist and friend of Elias Ashmole, founder of the Ashmolean collection. Dwight and Hooke had worked as assistants in Robert Boyle's laboratory in the High Street, Oxford (1656-60), where they gained much practical knowledge of chemistry, for Boyle was regarded as the founder of modern chemistry.

Hooke was to become curator of experiments to the Royal Society in 1663. Dwight took over John Fox's lease in Fulham, London; Fox had been Ashmole's servant (1648-1652) and subsequently ran a tavern so Dwight may have learnt of the site through his Oxford connections. This property and the adjoining site were to become the Fulham Pottery.

Ten years later, (1673-4) Dwight attended the House of Lords, with representatives of the London glass-sellers and tin-glaze earthenware potters, who respectively opposed and supported a proposed prohibition on imports of pottery. He is reported as saying that he could make 'as good and as much Cologne ware as would supply England'.

The only certain Dwight vessels excavated in Oxford include two bottles with a sprig moulded cock medallion and initials 'H.C.', recovered during the digging on the north side of the Radcliffe Camera and during excavations at the New Bodleian (Fig. 19). Another bottle with a medallion enclosing the letters R F M and one with initials RM were also found. E. T. Leeds, the assistant keeper at the Ashmolean (see Part II) believed that they were made for Roger and Mary Fowler. Fowler was a cook at St Alban's Hall and in the 1670s kept a cook-shop in Oxford, in nearby Catte Street, which was frequented by the incomparable Anthony Wood, a local historian and antiquarian, who knew both Plot and Ashmole.

E. T. Leeds wrote a paper entitled 'A Possible link with Samuel Pepys' and suggested that the H. C. medallion excavated from the underground bookstore site of the Radcliffe Camera should probably be associated with the Henry Crosse who kept the Cock

Fig. 18. A hand-modelled bust of John Dwight; chemist, potter and entrepreneur. A magnificent sculpture dated *c*.1673–5. Courtesy of Victoria and Albert Museum.

Tavern at Temple Bar, London, and in 1655 issued a trade token with a cock emblem and his initials and those of his wife.

Seventeenth-century scientists were intrigued by the secrets of porcelain manufacture. Hooke was aware that Dwight was experimenting with the imitation of 'China-Ware' and Plot wrote of the enterprising Dwight: 'He discovered the "secret of making *Earth* white and transparent as Porcellane", to this *Earth* he hath added the colours that are usual in the colour'd *China-Ware*'. He clearly was well informed and impressed by Dwight's experiments: 'He hath also caused to be modelled *Statues* or *Figures* of the said transparent *Earth* (a thing not done elsewhere, for *China* affords us only imperfect *mouldings*)... In short, he has so far advanced *Art Plastick*, that 'tis dubious whether any man since *Prometheus* have excelled *him* not except the *Damophilus*, and *Gorgsus* of Pliny'. Plot, resident Professor of Chemistry at Oxford and known to some as 'old Pluto' may have gained his up-to-date information through the Royal Society of London for Improving Natural Knowledge, where he and Hooke were actively involved, or directly from Dwight himself. In his topographical survey, Plot mentions the making of 'Models, Gargills or Anticks'

Fig. 19. Wheel-thrown English stoneware tavern bottle with sprig-moulded medallion of cockerel and initials 'H.C.' and another with initials 'R. M.' made at the Fulham Pottery, London during Dwight's teneur. Only four bottles certainly from Fulham have been excavated in Oxford. Second half of seventeenth century. Radcliffe Square 1915.55 and 49. (Ht. 22 cm.; incomplete).

from the excellent white pipe clay of Shotover. Could this be where Dwight got his initial inspiration for making white stoneware figurines? Or was it at Wigan a regional centre of pottery making in north-west England, where he resided after he had left Oxford, that his keen interest was awakened? Dwight himself said he used pipe-clay for his statuettes; his second patent (1684) mentions the discovery of the mystery of 'transparent Porcellane'.

Dwight's remarkable achievement gained him a place amongst the important figures in the history of ceramics. He was a 'brilliant ceramic innovator, comparable with Josiah Wedgewood in the eighteenth century'. His experimental soft-paste porcelains and his white stoneware statues and figurines were probably the first attempts in northern Europe, which as ceramics are 'unique in the development of European baroque sculpture'.

The seventeenth century saw Oxford at its most dynamic and it was into this environment that Dwight was drawn; two generations later this energy had transferred itself from the University to the town, with an emphasis on consumer power.

This potential market hungry for the latest fashions and luxury goods caught the attention of a European craftsman.

— PORTRAIT —

Gilder, Potter and Rogue: J. Brolliet

Jacques Louis Brolliet, a Swiss by birth was a gilder who visited England on at least two occasions. On his first visit spending some time in Oxford. From a glowing letter of introduction written at a later date (1759) by the chemist Jean Hellot, a member of the *Academie*, to the Director of the Sèvres factory in France, we learn much of Broillet's supposed activities while in England. The letter states that Brolliet 'gilds porcelain well and quickly with gold leaves and with powdered gold. His mordant (a substance used to fix gold leaf) is not known at Sèvres... He could paint 20 decorative designs in monochrome a day'. He also learned the secrets of the soft paste porcelain being manufactured at Chelsea, widely regarded as the best early English porcelain, where the factory specialised in porcelain toys. Brolliet certainly visited the premises and may have worked there.

The letter outlines the complete manufacturing process 'in use at the "Oxford" salt-glazed stoneware pottery' at Oseney Mill, Oxford (Fig. 20). The preparation of the paste using 'terre de pipe' dug one mile from Oxford (Plot's Shotover source?), the glazing of the pots, the saggars to protect them in the kiln, and finally the actual firing is clearly set out. The Oxford kiln was apparently similar to that of Chelsea, which was modelled on the Staffordshire tradition. Coal was used as the fuel, although elsewhere wood was burnt. The Mill, situated on the river Thames, was slightly upstream from the wharves at Folly Bridge where produce was traditionally loaded or unloaded.

Confirmation comes in an advertisement placed by James Brolliet, Proprietor of the China Manufactory at Oseney Mill near Oxford on 11th January 1755.

'Proprietor of the China Manufactory at Oseney Mill near Oxford.

In order to convince the Publick that the scandalous and malicious Reports which have been propagated to his Prejudice are without the least Foundation,

Hereby begs leave to inform Gentlemen and Ladies, That he will burn China of his own making at Oseney Mill aforesaid, on Wednesday next the Fifteenth of the

Fig. 20. An engraving by Michael Burghers showing the range of domestic buildings adjoining the mill-stream at Oseney in 1720. Was this the location of Brolliet's firing in 1755? Courtesy of Bodleian Library.

Instant, from Nine o'clock in the Morning till Twelve, where all those who are pleased to honour him with their Company will receive proper Satisfaction.

N.B. Gentlemen and Ladies are desired not to handle the China before it is burnt.

A further document of January 25th 1755 states:

'Gentlemen and Ladies who are desirous of seeing a specimen of the China made by James Brolliet at Oseney near Oxford, are desired to apply to Mr. Bernard Gayse, Confectioner behind All Saints Church (now Lincoln College Library); where they will receive proper satisfaction that the scandalous reports which have spread by some evil-minded Persons, are malicious and groundless, and that this China is, absolutely of his own Manufactory'.

Nothing more is known of this enterprise from the local rents or documents of the period but Gayse like Brolliet may have originated from the Continent. Brolliet's knowledge of Dwight's white salt-glaze stoneware figurines may have been gleaned while in London or even in Oxford.

Further documents in France cast doubt on Brolliet's integrity as a potter. One year later he was working as a chemist in Canada, for the military commander. He returned to England c.1758 for a few months, then went back to France and worked as a servant to the academic Hellot, whose testimonial enabled him to enter the Sèvres factory in 1759. Documents from the Sèvres archives show him working in the *atelier de peinture* with a note '[his salary] must not be reduced; he brought to the factory the secret of transfer-printing'. Yet six months later he was sacked from the Sèvres factory (1760).

The transfer-printing technique was invented in Liverpool in the 1750's, after seeing children sticking waste prints onto broken earthenware to make doll's tea sets, and Brolliet had mastered the techniques of working with engraved copper plates while in London, perhaps from the famous French engraver, Ravenat. The plausible Brolliet continued to find patrons throughout his working life in France and Switzerland, but none of these working relationships lasted very long and perhaps 'point to a tumultuous private life'. From further documents, we learn that Brolliet considered the best white pottery in England to be that in Staffordshire. There were French connections with Staffordshire c.1730s when Ralph Shaw, a working potter, went to France, and some of his family returned in 1750.

Brolliet was also familiar with the technique of 'slip casting' which spread from Staffordshire to the rest of England in the 1740s.

Whether a 'China' kiln existed at Oxford will have to be tested by archaeologists in future — the month of January is an inclement month for firing a kiln. What is more certain is that Brolliet was adept at absorbing new ceramic technologies, shameless in his use of these innovations, and although for some reason he was not sufficiently industrious to make them profitable to himself, his career demonstrates the ease and speed with which new advances in technology could spread across Europe at this time.

The different methods of manufacture adopted by the potters are in part dictated by the clay, but are also tied to preferences for certain technologies which in turn reflect individual craftsmen — their patrons, their consumers and their local economies. Substantial technological changes in production took place between the end of the Roman period and the nineteenth century.

Stylistic Developments from the Ninth to the Nineteenth Century

The impact of modern archaeological studies on the material collected by the Antiquities Department over three centuries has been considerable. The technological and stylistic changes over time helps reconstruct the historic environment and provides new insights linking people and their cultures with local, regional, national and international economies.

With the demise of the Roman Empire, well-organised pottery industries failed and the art of the potter's wheel was lost to the British Isles. Immigrants from north Germany brought with them their own traditions of hand-made pots. Some of these, in particular the funerary pots, were clearly the work of very gifted craftsmen.

Ninth–Eleventh Century Oxford

From at least the ninth to the mid eleventh century, hand-made pots made with shelly clay from the Jurassic belt were favoured by the local potters.

The popularity of this fabric may be tied to firing. The limestone fragments would have the advantage of acting as a fluxing agent when heated over 650 C and thus lowering the temperature of maturity. The

Fig. 22. Hand-made earthenware cook or storage jar. Tenth-eleventh century. Hertford College City Ditch 1909.907. (Ht. 14 cm.).

temperature must nevertheless have been kept below 850 C, the temperature at which calcium carbonate disassociates, leaving the finished pot unstable. Pottery such as this would have been fired in a kiln with no permanent structure.

The wide diffusion of this ceramic tradition as far as London and Essex to the east, and smaller quantities to the west, in the West Midlands, suggests a well organised communications network by the tenth century at least. The distribution to the West Midlands, may be linked to salt trade, salt was much prized for preserving as well as enhancing the flavour of food.

Oxford, like other towns would have had a market for the sale of food — some perhaps in pots, livestock and other goods, which was probably centred on Carfax, the crossroads at the centre of Oxford. Although the potters were producing a narrow range of forms, many of these styles remained unchanged for generations; but for the consumers the function may have been of prime concern, rather than fashion.

Amongst the hand-made pottery of the period there are better crafted wares. Under the protection of the Scandanavians — the great technocrats and trading entrepreneurs — the potter's wheel was being reintroduced to this country from the Continent during the second half of the ninth century. Potters settled within the fortified towns of East Anglia, as at Thetford and in the East Midlands, such as Stamford.

Fig. 21. Hand-made earthenware burial urn, decorated with bosses and burnished lines and stamped impressions, recorded in Dr. Plot's catalogue. Fifth-sixth century. Tradescant Collection. Mus. Trad. 1685 Cat. B682. (Ht. 22 cm. incomplete).

Fig. 23. Map of England showing the extent of the Danelaw territory (stippled area).

grace earthen floors or the table were always glazed with a transparent lead glaze coloured green or yellow from the impurities in the clay and the amount of oxygen present in the firing of the pots. This technique spread from the Rhineland in Northern Germany. Recently pottery kilns have been located in an area of the Meuse valley which was also well known for its metal working; the spouted pitchers from these kilns are undoubtedly the precursors to those made at Stamford. Such vessels are represented in small numbers on almost all Oxford late Saxon sites, dating from the mid eleventh century and on through the twelfth century. This tradition was also traded widely across England.

The Stamford production centre was also responsible for manufacturing the majority of the crucibles found in Oxford, such vessels were traded throughout the Midlands and to the north of England (Fig. 26).

These potters were familiar with metal technology and this enabled them to develop the appropriate ceramic containers for metal smelting. The estuarine clay, with its low iron and high silica content is little affected by the high temperatures, *c.*1100 C, necessary for working with copper alloys, gold or silver. This same clay was also used for domestic vessels, although few have been excavated from the town, in comparison with the number of crucibles.

The remarkable state of preservation of the crucibles recovered from 18-20 Cornmarket Street, in the busy central north street, set this assemblage apart. The majority of the vessels are thumb-pot crucibles. Similar thumb-pots were found on the site of the Old Angel Inn, on the main east axis to the town, but not in such quantities. Wheel-thrown bag-shaped and

These towns lay within the 'Danelaw', an area established by treaty separating the Danes from the English (Fig. 23).

Elaborate trading networks, seem to have reached as far west as the Oxford region, although politically the region lay outside the Danelaw. This is indicated by St. Neot's ware, which saturated the South Midlands and extended as far north as York.

St. Neots ware vessels show the confident technical innovation of these craftsmen, specialising in fine-walled wheel-thrown pots (Fig. 24).

Initially only used by some households locally, by the mid eleventh century they were adopted by the full range of society. The capacity of these pots was in the range of three to five pints, smaller than the local wares. Such widespread distribution of St. Neot's and St. Neot's types would imply considerable economic and even cultural stability despite the Viking raids of the tenth and eleventh century, under firm administrative control probably at a number of points: Oxford, a large fortified town and a major commercial centre, could have provided such a point.

The next technical innovation followed rapidly — fine pale estuarine clays near Stamford in south Lincolnshire were used to throw the first spouted pitchers. Visually splendid, these powerful symbols designed to

Fig. 24. Line drawing of a wheel-thrown earthenware cook pot or serving vessel of St. Neot's-type ware – one of the major ceramic traditions of the Saxo-Norman period. Mid tenth-mid eleventh century. Clarendon Hotel 1958 (Ht. 20 cm. Scale 1:4).

Fig. 25. Wheel-thrown earthenware pitcher with lead glaze, made in Stamford, south Lincolnshire. This was one of the vessels dispersed shortly after it was dug up and later presented to the British Museum by A. W. Franks, a friend of Arthur Evan's father, John Evans (see later Inferences for Medieval Oxford's Heritage). Eleventh-twelfth century. Old Angel Inn. (Ht. 17 cms). Courtesy of the Trustees of the British Museum.

hemisperical pots of Stamford type were more common from the St. Ebbe's excavations in the south-west of the town, and may post-date those found in the commercial centre. An isolated crucible from the Radcliffe Camera excavations in 1909 contained traces of copper and 'gold' adhering to the vessel.

Vitrification occurs on the inner surface of most of these pots — crucible slag, formed by the reaction of fuel ash and metal oxides from the melt, combine with the crucible fabric. Traces of metal are contained in many of them, either as discrete droplets of greenish copper, or as a residue of bright red. Only one vessel was unused. A larger vessel was found in association with the smaller thumb-pots.

Copper-red areas on crucibles may also indicate silver and gold working, since precious metals usually contained some copper. Although seven moneyers were working in Oxford in the tenth and eleventh century, it has never been established where these mints were located. A range of continental imports, from northern France, the Rhineland and Belgium occur, suggest widening contact with the Continent, as merchants exported wool and cloth and imported luxury goods and wine, underpinned by increasing economic and political stability. This in turn correlates with the documented evidence for royal councils meeting in Oxford during the second decade of the eleventh century.

By the mid eleventh century, a generation before the Norman Conquest in 1066, the shelly wares had been replaced by different clay sources: one with naturally occuring flint, another with naturally occurring calcareous gravel. Slightly later, a third source, with sand added by the potters to improve the clay, made an impact in the region. More significantly, the art of the wheel was lost to the region — the indigeneous potters reasserted themselves with their handmaking techniques. It was to be several generations before the wheel was reintroduced again into the region, a trend replicated across much of south east Midlands. There was, therefore, no continuity of the technical skills.

These indigenous potters from Mercia and to a less extent from Wessex introduced their own protojug — a cooking pot with tubular spout, to join the limited repertoire of cooking and storage vessels, shallow pans and lamps. These proto-jug shapes can always be distinguished by the stamped decoration around the shoulders of pots (Fig. 27). The size of the cook pot and storage jars also changed and increased three-fold. Contemporary ethnographic studies show it is difficult to relate pot size to the standard of living, poor people often eat food of high bulk. This change in the capacity of the vessels suggests some re-arrangement of the social organisation within individual households. This change is mirrored throughout much

Fig. 26. Pinch pot earthenware crucibles made in Stamford, south Lincolnshire. Tenth-eleventh century.

of England and northern Europe. In the Low Countries it has been suggested that several people now ate from the same pot, using a piece of bread to convey food to their mouths.

Twelfth–Thirteenth Century Oxford

With the demise of St. Neot's, the ceramic networks became very localised and by the early twelfth century may have been under the control of local magnates, who were no longer Saxon but of Norman origin. Ideas can spread very rapidly, as seen with the adoption of glaze technology across southern England. Two glazed traditions emerged locally and provided tablewares for both the urban and rural consumer during the twelfth and early thirteenth century.

The robust tripod pitcher, a decanter for wine or ale, was designed to sit on a flat surface (Fig. 28). It was visually pleasing and suggests an improvement in the quality of life and a certain affluence — the leisure to sit at table, graced with decorative tablewares or perhaps the broadening of this lifestyle to a wider range of people. Less common was the smaller jug with tubular spout, possibly used as a drinking jug. The introduction of decoration during this period coincided with the embellishment of Romanesque architecture; both used applied structural decoration, pilaster strips on buildings are matched by applied strips on pots, sometimes alternating red and white. The applied and thumbed strips and plaited decoration on handles may also be skeuomorphic designs of rope containers or basketry. The decoration of utilitarian vessels also implies a more stable and prosperous economy was enjoyed by some of the major

Fig. 28. Hand-made earthenware tripod pitchers, also a small spouted pitcher stylistically similar to the larger vessel suggesting it was made by the same potter. All these vessels were made in the same production centre to the north of Oxford. Twelfth-thirteenth century.

pottery workshops, which in turn was stimulated by the consumer.

Not only had the producers mastered the improved technology which was required to achieve a glaze (i.e more controlled firing), but they also had the confidence to buy in new commodities: iron-rich clay, iron-free clay for the decorative slip and lead galena. The lead galena was not only decorative but also improved the function, by better retaining liquid. Lead galena had to be imported long distances from either the Mendips, or possibly Cornwall or Derbyshire. This would have necessitated considerable interaction with middlemen, who supplied these new commodities; some potters at least were now competing with market forces and their social role in the community was beginning to change.

The preference for sand tempering may be allied to the introduction of lead galena on pottery. This new technology may in turn be associated with the making of ecclesiastical stained glass, which also relied heavily on the use of sand. Was their introduction related to the Norman influences more familiar with glaze technology, or to the development of stained glass as a decorative art? At the periphery of the region, away from new patronage, the potter's world

Fig. 27. Line drawing of hand-made earthenware proto-jug with stamp decoration, made to the west and south-west of Oxford. Eleventh-twelfth century. Radcliffe Square 1915.9a. (Ht. 20cm., Scale 1:4).

Fig. 29. Hand-made and wheel-thrown earthenware jugs and pitchers from several production centres: a shelly ware made to the east of Oxford on the Northamptonshire/Bedfordshire border (left), 'painted' wares to the south, from central Berkshire, and iron-free white wares probably from the coal measures in the Midlands (centre and right). Late twelfth-early thirteenth century.

was possibly a tougher, starker place, and some traditions did not adopt the new glaze technology.

The growth of Oxford's academic community from the middle of the twelfth century, which co-incided with a national demographic explosion, would have increased the town's population as well as embracing *alumni* from the Continent. The pottery population increased also — a wider range of sizes of cooking pots and storage vessels was now introduced — suggesting yet again a change in consumer requirements. The diet remained unchanged however: pottage, a soup-like stew was still eaten daily by everyone. The spouted pitchers gave way to medieval pitchers with pinched lips and may suggest a shift from drinking directly from the pitcher to a more personalised drinking vessel, perhaps made of wood.

New innovations were added to the potter's repertoire: a variety of ceramic lamps for lighting dark corners of dwellings were made. Curfews (firecovers) were introduced: their function was to sustain the embers overnight to avoid the necessity of re-kindling the fire each morning, and to ensure that sparks were contained

when the fire was not in use. Their introduction to the ceramic repertoire may indicate a heightening of communal responsibility in matters concerning safety, and was also a pragmatic response to keeping live coals alight. Manning collected portable ceramic lamps of all periods in the 1890's, including tall pedestal and spiked cresset lamps, types which copied Saxon glass prototypes which are portrayed in contemporary illuminated manuscripts.

The founding of the late twelfth-century market towns probably gave a new stimulus to the existing ceramic industries, who could then risk their merchandise travelling further and be assured of a demand at some more distant market. The creation of specific market days at each market town would have further improved an itinerary for the middleman, and thus encouraged a degree of industrialization. Fairs were also important in the exchange of goods, such as St. Frideswide, a fair at Oxford, whose feast was in July from the end of the eleventh century, but by the beginning of the thirteenth century had moved to October. The profits formed part of the King's annual revenue in the early twelfth century. The King's court often stayed at Beaumont Palace (west of the Ashmolean) on their way to the favoured royal hunting lodge at Woodstock, eight miles north of Oxford. Historical evidence shows that courts were notorious consumers and their visits would further have stimulated the need for pottery vessels and containers, if only as decanters of ale or wine.

The population continued to grow, as seen by the infilling of the areas later associated with the Old Angel Inn, New Bodleian and Radcliffe Camera (see Part II). A wider variety of regional imports, principally serving jugs and pitchers often decorated with a masterly sense of design, is evident through to the early thirteenth century (Fig. 29).

The introduction of tolls levied on goods entering the town may have favoured the more commercial pottery producers for selling in the market place. By the later twelfth century the smaller regional networks were being replaced by just a few potteries, probably situated within or at the edges of forests, on land that would never have yielded a good agricultural crop. These were to develop into the major potteries of the thirteenth–fifteenth centuries.

Native craftsmen centred on Minety in north Wiltshire and in the environs of the Savernake Forest of East Wiltshire supplied much of west and south-west Oxfordshire with utilitarian products for both the urban and rural consumer: large cooking pots, storage vessels, jugs, firecovers and deep-sided bowls or pans (Fig. 30). Later bung-hole jars were added to their repertoire.

The Savernake Forest jars were coil made unglazed coarse wares, but had an astonishing distribution, suggesting an aggressive marketing strategy which, in part, may be related to the local rural economy, in this case, dairy farming. This technically unsophisticated ware, with clay and coarse flint and chalk inclusions, lent itself to the perpetual expansion and contraction endured during the heating and cooling down processes associated with cooking and warming milk, and for making of butter, curds and cheese. The open texture may also have retained bacteria more readily, which would hasten the curdling of milk to make yoghurt and cheese in wide shallow pans.

This conservative ceramic tradition continued in use to the sixteenth century.

Thirteenth–Fourteenth Century Oxford

Pottery is a commodity. The prices of individual items are rare at this period, but a substantial order for 4,500 cups from the hunting lodge/palace at Woodstock in 1267, costing £2 13s. 7°d. may have been directed to the prolific workshops at Brill/Boarstall (assuming the cups were made from pottery and not wood). An inventory for a dairy at the moated manor at Hampstead

Fig. 30. Coil made earthenware vessels from Minety in north Wiltshire and Savernake Forest were probably transported to market by cart. Late twelfth-fifteenth century. Swindon; no accession no.; Radcliffe Square 1915.268a. (Ht. 25 cm.; 33 cm.).

Marshall, in neighbouring Berkshire shows that in 1297-9, two pots and six pans cost 3*d*. The price of an individual pot was therefore not cheap, given that an average man was earning about 1*d*. per day, the equivalent to two loaves of bread or four pints of ale.

Some people clearly thought it worthwhile to mend their pots with plugs of lead; several examples of this thrift occur in the region.

The Production Centre

'Brill on the hill, where the wind blows chill'.

Brill with its magnificent views across Oxfordshire and Buckinghamshire, was a favoured place in the medieval period. Edward the Confessor had a hunting lodge there. Later, Brill was host to the court of two medieval kings: during the reign of Henry III (1230-70), a member of the house of Anjou or Plantagenant, eighty nine tuns of wine were consumed at the hunting lodge. The wine arrived in wooden tuns: most of it came from Southampton, but thirteen tuns were brought from the King's cellars in Oxford and four from London. One could speculate that this wine would have been in need of decanting, creating a need for ceramic jugs and pitchers to draw the wine from the casks. The ready market of the court and all its retainers may be the key to the location of the potteries, which were also close to the fuel and raw materials.

The patronage of a king would have enabled the potters to develop their craft and to experiment technically and artistically in the making of elaborate finewares, initiatives which were to place their wares amongst the finest in southern England. Such patronage was unusual in England. It was during the period of the Barons Revolt (1258-66) that Oxford was in 'the forefront of national affairs' and the increased wealth may also have stimulated the craftsmen to decorate everyday objects more lavishly.

Some potters were probably working at Brill by the end of twelfth century. The earliest pottery attributed to Brill is of a coarse open fabric, reminiscent of Minety or Wychwood traditions, found to the west of Oxford and very different from the later and better-known

Fig. 31. Wheel-thrown earthenware innovations from the Brill/Boarstall workshops: small cook pots/serving vessels, bottles partially glazed and shelled lamps with glossy green or mottled green glaze on the cup and drip tray. Lighting was a luxury in any medieval household. Thirteenth century.

finewares. This, together with vessel forms, give some support to the hypothesis that the earliest potters may have been influenced by, or may even have originated from, the Bristol hinterland. Masons from the Severn Valley were working in Oxford some years previously; and influences from the west continued to dominate the ceramic market in Oxford until the sixteenth century.

Pottery making at Brill was first mentioned in an inquisition in 1254. However it was around the 1230s, that potters deliberately added sand to improve the clay, and threw their pots competently on a fast wheel, the first instance of its use since the demise of St. Neot's in the mid eleventh century. Cooking pots, storage jars and bowls were produced, the potters specialising in smaller sized vessels than many of their competitors, catering for the individual rather than the family unit.

Shelled lamps and bottles in a variety of sizes, used as containers for oils and sauces for culinary use, were new innovations to the region (Fig. 31). Wide, shallow pans are absent, perhaps because the producers were not supplying the agricultural community or because such vessels were made of wood. The outstanding quality of jugs and pitchers as decanters and drinking vessels, reflected the taste and fashions of the day. The tablewares were skilfully decorated, some with rilling on the neck reminiscent of French jugs (see Fig. 58) — a characteristic also paralleled on Bristol type jugs.

The stimulus for these subjects and symbols may be derived from life in the forest — the environment around the craftworkers — but also from textiles, leather-work, wrought iron-work, stained glass and architectural detail, influenced by all iconography associated with the church. Visual imagery was of fundamental importance and the medieval mind was adept at interpreting everything symbolically. Slip decoration, rouletting using roller stamps in a variety of combinations, applied pellets of clay, grid-stamped pads were all employed to create beautiful jugs (Fig. 32).

Pads with comical faces also occur. Some of the scroll decoration with terminals of red iron-rich clay represent the flowers and fruits of the vine, a design often found on stone carvings and painted stained glass. Others were clearly influenced by the floral and foliage motifs on ironwork, which are similar to the decorative iron scrolls at St. George's Chapel, Windsor, dated 1240-49, and at Notre Dame in Paris.

Baluster types derived from wooden prototypes, or from tall leather jacks which in turn copy the

Fig. 32. Wheel-thrown earthenware decorative jugs and pitchers illustrating the variety and vitality of the thirteenth century potters at the Brill/Boarstall workshops in central Buckinghamshire. The reintroduction of the wheel enabled the potters to meet the needs of the growing urban communities.

architectural columns of the same name continued throughout the medieval period (see Fig. 57). Several balusters were rescued by T. E. Lawrence and his school friend C. F. Beeson (see Part II) from the site of the Civet Cat (No. 7 Cornmarket Street), one from the shaft of a well some 27ft. down. It is clear that the potters had been copying French jugs, with their modelling of parrot beak spouts so common on the export polychrome Saintonge vessels from south west France. The Saintonge potters also threw their handles on the wheel but there is no evidence that this technique was adopted at local workshops. As we have seen much of the original inspiration for the Brill/Boarstall workshops came from France, either via Bristol or possibly through direct contact.

Jugs and pitchers from the Brill/Boarstall kilns form a large component of the vessels recovered from the famous collection of the New Bodleian, Oxford in 1930s. Bruce-Mitford, as a young graduate (see Part II) arranged them into the first typological series of medieval jugs, showing their progressive development, a series which is substantially correct even today for the local types. But there were some gaps in the sequence which can now be filled for the mid thirteenth century, including the highly decorated stout baluster types, decorated baluster types and triple-decker vessels, which are often outstanding examples of decorative art.

The magnificent triple-decker was unique to the Brill/Boarstall production centre, and a wide variety of plastic decoration is found on this type of vessel. Only half a dozen such vessels have been excavated from Oxford and may represent the work of just one workshop.

Puzzle-jugs for drinking games — a pastime continued into the nineteenth century — were thrown in two parts at this period, reflecting the ingenuity of the potter. One exuberant example acquired by Manning from the site of the Town Hall was elaborately decorated with clay pellets representing the leaves of the forest, with a stag's head with splendid antlers peering through the foliage, and with human faces around the top of the rim.

Manning's jug was found in the Jewish quarter of Oxford and almost certainly represents a commemorative jug made as a special masterpiece. It illustrates the consummate skill and imagination of the potter, and parallels a sister vessel from the site of the Old Angel Inn now held by the British Museum. T. E. Lawrence recognised that they were almost certainly made by the same craftsman.

Other light-hearted anthropomorphic jugs may have belonged to puzzle-jugs or to spouted jugs. Aquamaniles copying metal prototypes were used for dispensing water at table for washing the hands, prior to taking food belong to this period (Fig. 33). Their ultimate ancestry may lie with the figurines of the Middle East and show that the conventual rules in personal behaviour were evolving, arising perhaps from a hightened consciousness by the wealthier inhabitants of the beneficial qualities of cleaness. This concept was familiar to Islam, and the introduction of hand washing to northern Europe may be linked with the Crusades. The potter's craft was highly regarded in Islamic countries, a very different attitude to that prevailing in England.

An astonishing variety of decorative styles was present by the mid thirteenth century; most of the

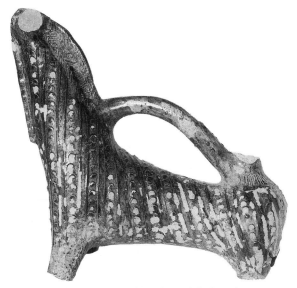

Fig. 33. A finely executed hand-modelled earthenware aquamanile, with incised and scale decoration covered with mottled green glaze. Such vessels may indicate new levels of hygience in some households. There are only two Oxford examples in the collection. Clarendon Hotel 1955.480. (Ht. 29 cm.).

applied decorative types were used on triple-deckers and stout baluster types, or the exotic puzzle-jugs and aquamaniles (Fig. 34). Such vessels were indicative of more ostentatious living, and the inspiration for their shapes and capacity may lie with pewter and silverware prototypes. These rapid changes suggest it was a period when fashion was readily assimilated by potter craftsman, who displayed considerable mental agility and were encouraged by their clientele to provide vigorous decoration. This trend is evident at many urban centres in England, and contemporary Paris also saw an astonishing flowering in the quality of its crafts.

The technical pioneering of the thirteenth century gave way to artisans manufacturing mass-produced pottery for a larger market — producing reasonable quality jugs. The fourteenth century was thus a period of adaptation and modification of existing techniques.

Fourteenth–Fifteenth Century Oxford

The transport of pots from the Brill/Boarstall production centre to market was probably effected by cart. Pots could be packed with bracken or straw in the body of the cart or suspended along its sides as depicted in the fourteenth century *Luttrell Psalter*. In Oxford there were two weekly street markets, held on Wednesdays and Saturdays, when craftsmen became vendors, with an extra market on Sundays at harvest time. Sellers of earthenware shared a stall with charcoal sellers in the High Street during the later fourteenth century, and these stalls may have included products from both Wiltshire and Buckinghamshire.

Potters sold their products to townsmen, countryfolk, merchants and officials of abbeys, who liked to buy in bulk: pots, platters and dishes for the Priors' Chamber at Bicester Priory in the north east of the county were purchased in 1346 at 3s. 7d.

On the west side of St. Aldates were the vendors of dishes and scullery ware, which were presumably of brass or other metals. Metal vessels begin to be mentioned more in household accounts, and in an effort to stem the competitive edge of the metalworkers, potters began to copy the expensive metal and metal-bound wooden vessels, with their angular bodies and deep grooves running round the circumference of the vessel (Figs 4 top left and 36 top left).

Copying metalwork resulted in plainer jugs with little applied structural decoration, although metal dies were sometimes used as stamps (Fig. 36b), a technique employed earlier on twelfth century painted glass. Vessel shapes had altered little since their inception but smaller drinking jugs and cylindrical mugs, some with face masks — possibly associated with the legend of the green man, a potent symbol in myths and religions around the world — were more in evidence. Mottled green was still the favoured glaze colour, suggesting the colour was all important: it may have symbolised prestige; as copper oxide had to be imported from south west France or north Africa; or the colour green may have symbolised fertility, renewal and growth.

The manor of Brill passed out of the king's direct control in 1324 and this, coupled with the economic depression of the 1330s which affected the volume of trade, may have contributed to the demise of this ceramic industry by the mid fourteenth century.

The reduction in Oxford's trade and population culminated in the riot which threatened the exist-

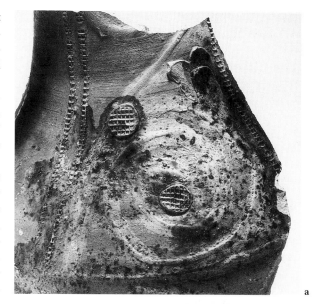

a

b

c

Fig. 34. **Medieval decorative motifs: a) the scroll derived from foliate designs was popular with other medieval craftsmen, applied white strips, sometimes roller-stamped with contrasting iron-rich red stamped pads; b) medieval brooches were a favourite motif at many production centres, applied strip in a circlet with applied stamped pads imitating semi-precious stones; c) the lozenge design showing stylistic links with contemporary stonework, glass and the magnificent wooden ceiling at Peterborough cathedral dated 1220.**

ence of the University. On St. Scholastica's Day, 10 February 1354/5, some clerks quarrelled with the liquor that the vintner offered them in the Swyndlestock Inn (see Part II). They used strong language and threw wine and a vessel at his head. The ensuing riot, following the Black Death must have affected consumer and producer alike.

The commercial prosperity of Oxford continued to decline in the fifteenth century. Ceramic collections such as that recovered from Stodley Inn beneath the London and County Bank in 1867 are small in comparison with earlier assemblages and there is very little independent dating for the end of the medieval period. Vacated properties were eagerly bought up by the colleges of the University whose allegiance still lay with the Pope. The potter's craft was also influenced by specific changes, the widespread and regular drinking of ale and the corresponding increase of the brewers — often widows in the town — were responsible for the production of small drinking jugs and the occasional waisted beaker, many of these were associated with academic halls and colleges. One large pot for storing ale or for carrying water was purchased by Magdalen College, cost as much as 4d. in 1481-2.

The potters continued to supply functional vessels without the decorative elements. In the fifteenth cen-

tury, a wider range of smaller tablewares, not copied by other traditions in the region, suggests that the Brill/Boarstall workshops were targeting the urban market, stimulating tastes for more imaginative presentation of food, linked perhaps to changes in diet, and that the urban community was continuing to demand ceramic copies of metal or wooden prototypes. The Surrey/Hampshire pottery industries to the south also developed small tablewares at this period so there may have been some contact between the two industries. Small shallow bowls reminiscent of earlier turned wood (treen) dishes traditionally used for drinking, and small cruets, were increasingly used for vinegars and sauces, possibly sold by wine merchants. Cruets, copying metal vessels, are traditionally believed to be associated with a religious function (Fig. 36 in the foreground). However, in Oxford archaeological deposits show them to be associated with domestic living. Small chafing dishes used to keep food warm at table suggest a change in some households in conventional table habits. Skillets for frying, baking dishes for catching the basting fluid from a joint turned on the spit; pottery lids to cover jars; and condiments designed for salt or spices at table were introduced. Ceremonial salts used at high table, often depicted in illuminated manuscripts, were originally

Fig. 35. The incident which sparked the town and gown riot is depicted in a fourteenth century manuscript of the Luttrell Psalter. Pots as weapons are a pictorial theme illustrated in northern Europe up to the seventeenth century. Courtesy of the British Library.

Fig. 36. Wheel-thrown earthenware drinking jugs and pitchers in a variety of sizes, with mottled green glaze; new late fourteenth century innovations: cylindrical mugs with face masks, smaller tablewares, cruets and barrel-shaped jugs; batch marks or merchant's marks as on the base of the shallow bowl (in the foreground, 36a) and the use of metal dyes to stamp pottery, an example can be seen on the handle of a fifteenth century jug (top shelf right, 36b).

in precious metal. One new shape of jug was introduced at this period locally: the barrel-shaped jug imitating metal-bound wooden tuns (Fig. 36 back row left on the table).

By the end of the fifteenth century Brill potters reverted to transparent glazes, and pots were finished with a 'bib' of glaze only, lead became too expensive (the lead industry was in decline and was considered an expensive building material at this time). More rarely there were pottery horns, perhaps used in hunting, similar to those known throughout northern Europe. Toys such as whistles and finally money boxes — known as thrift boxes or apprentice boxes, were novelties added to the potter's repertoire, and the concept spread rapidly to all parts of England. Thrift boxes continued to be made up to the present century — a novelty that clearly captured the consumer's imagination! The products suggest that the potters were searching for new markets away from the kitchen and table. But ceramic pots continued to be used for cooking even though metal cauldrons were increasingly popular. Coarse wares from the west of Oxfordshire, from Minety in Wiltshire and from the Savernake Forest area still had a place.

Some earlier forms continued and it is clear that there were renewed periods of economic distress in the fifteenth century where potting skills were sometimes very inferior to those employed during the second half of the thirteenth century. Nonetheless, these empty vessels still found a market. Overall the spending power of the consumer grew enabling them to buy a wider range of purchases.

The strong regional preferences were also beginning to be eroded, as the local variations in the shape of the basic medieval product of cook pot, jug and bowls were replaced by shapes which were replicated throughout southern England. Well glazed drinking cups and mugs, that were pleasant to use, began to be adopted over a wide swathe of England, suggesting the rapid spread of ideas, not seen since the adoption of glazed pitchers in the twelfth century.

However, products from the Surrey/Hampshire border were beginning to break the local monopoly long enjoyed by the Brill/Boarstall workshops. These iron-free products were to increase gradually throughout the post-medieval period, suggesting that the Brill potteries were no longer in the hands of middlemen or entrepreneurs and were probably without strong corporate leadership.

Individual items from the Rhineland began to find their way inland. The earliest salt-glazed stonewares recovered from Oxford were rescued by Arthur Evans, from King Edward Street. These Raeren-type funnel-necked jugs, copying Siegburg shapes possibly dating to late fifteenth century, have only been found on this site and at Carfax (Glyn Mills site and see Part II a Portrait of A. J. Evans), although there was contact with a German merchant in 1463 and a steady trade in imported wine.

Sixteenth Century Tudor Oxford

A new visual language was necessary to represent the shift from a medieval world, which was based on the Christian culture of God and heaven when all human activity was judged from a moral point of view, to one based on nature and antiquity. It was a period where humanity became the centre of all things — on the Continent some craftspeople including potters were recognised as artists and art was regarded as a brand of science, resulting in the visualisation of science.

The new stimulus from Flemish potters and craftsmen settling in Tudor England, in East Anglia and London, did not however reach inland to Oxfordshire and Buckinghamshire until the end of the century; new modes of interior decoration such as lighting and heating technology (ornamental brick hearths and ceramic tile stoves) did not play a significant part in Oxford's interiors. Manning's collection includes the only glazed stove tile dredged from a stream south of Grandpont, Oxford.

The local medieval industries were contracting; the important cloth and leather workshops had declined markedly and the population in the town at the beginning of the century was below 3,000, mostly craftsmen and shopkeepers. The archaeological ceramic

Fig. 37. An engraving after Breughal by Pieter van der Heyden, published 1570 AD. Gardener's at work, with pots in ceramic, baskets of wicker and wooden buckets. Douce Bequest. 209 x 285 image.

assemblages for this period are still very small. The local ceramic industry centred on Brill limped into the sixteenth century, modifications to the medieval tradition of jug-making continuing to be influenced by metal prototypes. Bung-hole jars, wide-mouthed higher-fired oxidised jars became more prevalent, perhaps indicating a shift towards storage and the preserving of foodstuffs. The Brill potters now added deep-sided flanged pans to the urban ceramic repertoire, which may have been used for washing clothes or in the preparation of food. These vessels had previously been supplied by potters to the west and south west of Oxford, but by the sixteenth century these potteries had virtually ceased trading, so leaving an opportunity for the Brill potters to fill the void.

Something of a minor social revolution was illustrated by the introduction of fine earthenware mugs and cups with clear lead glazes in the Cistercian style, arising from the new firing technology of the late fifteenth century when saggars, designed to protect small vessels in the kiln, had been invented (Fig. 38). These drinking vessels continued to gain momentum (replacing the earlier treen cups of the medieval period) in tandem with an increase in the brewing trade and earthenware bung-hole jars.

Larger charcoal-burning chafing dishes were in use, and lobed bowls 'Tudor Green' with attractive bright green and mottled green glazes, were possibly passed around for drinking (Fig. 39). The attractive bright green glaze used on very fine 'Tudor Green' is found on very few sites in Oxford, and may indicate households of some standing, because 'ashen and green pots' (presumably the green glazed pots) are mentioned at an election banquet in London in 1522 A.D.

These English wares were supplemented by tin-glaze earthenware ring vases, from either the Netherlands or Italy (Fig. 40). They sometimes have the sacred monogram 'IHS', the abbreviation of the name of Jesus in Greek, and are often depicted in paintings of the period, for instance in a late Flemish Book of Hours — a personal calendar of prayers — in the Douce Collection (see Part II for a Portrait of Jackson). Such flower vases or 'altar vases' have been excavated from early collegiate layers, from the suburbs as well as from the University area, and were clearly cherished by a wide range of society. The presence of such ring vases may also have some religious overtones in the unsettled sixteenth century. These ring vases together with fine cups and mugs suggest changing social perceptions, a population with leisure to imbide, to enjoy nature and with a visual

Fig. 38. **Wheel-thrown smaller earthenware jugs with 'bibs' of glaze, glazed drinking cups, apprentice boxes and hand-made condiments indicate a shift in consumer demand. Rhenish stoneware drinking vessels begin to move inland. Sixteenth century.**

awareness that may owe something to the new learning of Renaissance Europe.

Despite the apparent improved hygiene at some tables, the quality of life for others was not markedly different from how it had been throughout the Middle Ages. The plague erupted repeatedly, Eramus, a Dutch scholar and great internationalist, visited Oxford early in the century and complained about the unhygenic conditions in English households. 'spitte, vomit and urine of dogs and men, beer... and other filth unmentionable was cast on the floor'. Archaeological evidence in the town gives a similarly earthy picture. The local authorities were concerned by unsanitary conditions, and local potters were stimulated to copy the continental watering pots used for dampening down the rushes on floors with their dust and filth (Fig. 41). The sprinkler types were used also for flowers (the latter use is illustrated in a tapestry dating to the fourteenth century displayed in the Cluny Museum, Paris) and an interest in horticulture emerged in some households (Fig. 37).

The human potential of the individual counted for more, and this is highlighted in a delightful *Schnelle* with applied panels depicting a full length portrait of Judith with the head of Holofernes, whom she beheaded to save her people (Fig. 43). Inspired by the biblical story depicted in contemporary printed books, it is a style unique in Oxford. This dated drinking vessel (1572), with an armorial medallion, was rescued from the site of the Old Angel Inn (see Part II); similar pots elsewhere in England are always associated with high status sites.

Fig. 39. Wheel-thrown finely potted earthenware tablewares from the Surrey/Hampshire Border production centres, decorated with mottled green glaze, and (left) a rare Rhenish stoneware costrel, a shape possibly inspired by vegetable gourds, much quoted in medieval and later literature. Costrels or travelling bottles were also made locally, possibly copying Rhenish prototypes.

Raeren stoneware mugs of a similar date with grey lead glaze were recovered from The Three Cups Inn, Queen Street and the city ditch on its northern side (Tredwell's Yard), next to the Leopold Arms (see Part II). These drinking mugs are typical of the type made famous by the Dutch painter, Breughel in his still life paintings of peasants carousing.

Years of bad harvests, added to the depression in the cloth industry and inflationary prices, must have affected everyone. The dissolution of the monastic orders in Oxford would have radically modified demand too. The Dominicans had placed large orders with the Brill/Boarstall workshops since the mid thirteenth century, and many students lived in houses maintained by religious orders.

Such disruption may have encouraged competent individuals formerly working at the Brill workshops to move out and start up independently elsewhere to find new markets, resulting in short-lived family concerns. Evidence of this is found at Combe, in north-

Fig. 40. Wheel-thrown tin-glaze earthenware ring vase, with gold 'IHS', a sacred monogram, painted on persian blue background. The colours are those of San Bernardino in Italy where such vessels are believed to be for export only. New Bodleian 1937.488. (Ht. 11cm.).

west Oxfordshire, close to Leafield, where research has recently shown wasters which were typologically and stylistically identical to Brill wares, but potted in a distinctive clay.

After 1570 life in England started to change. The appetite of the upper echelons for luxury goods does perhaps owe something to the new learning and books on etiquette were more widely available. The spending power of the ordinary consumer seems to expand enabling the consumer to make a wide range of purchases, as seen by the variety of ceramic utensils in the inventories of the period. Locally the population was growing, and the wealthy sent their sons to University to learn to be gentlemen. The ceramic products had to compete with a broader range of consumer goods: pewter and glass in particular, and leather black jacks were still used in taverns and colleges during the sixteenth and seventeenth centuries.

Stoneware bottles with naturalistic faces, flowing beard, rounded belly and moulded coat of arms were imported from the Rhineland. The arms of Cologne, Amsterdam and Queen Elizabeth I are all represented. A dated stoneware '1556' was rescued from the University area and two other dated examples (1594) were found at sites of two inns in the commercial centre (the area behind the Civet Cat in Cornmarket, belonging to the Cross and Roebuck Inns and the Fleur-de-Luce in St. Aldate's see Part II). The date '1594' recurs repeatedly on Rhenish stonewares in this country but cannot be related to any known historical event and may reflect the date of production.

Other bearded stone pots with applied relief decoration of portrait medallions, acanthus leaf designs and inscribed legends on the waist-bands were probably inspired by contemporary woodcuts (Fig. 42).

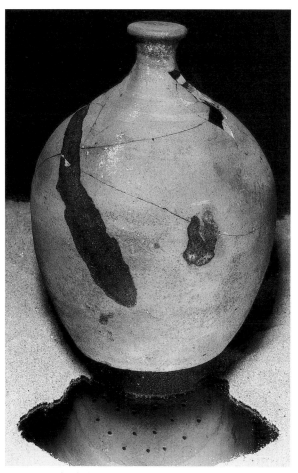

Fig. 41. **Wheel-thrown red earthenware watering sprinkler. The method of using these pots was to immerse the perforated base in water and then place the thumb over the hole at the top, to retain the water by creating a vacuum. These pots may have had a dual purpose and were on occasions used to dampen down the rushes to lay the dust. Sixteenth/seventeenth century. Radcliffe Square 1915.39. (Ht. 22cm.).**

Fig. 42. **German cartouches : 'Drink and Eat but forget not God'; 'What God wants is your soul' and 'Drink and eat but forget not the poor' (inverted). Only half a dozen such legends have been excavated in Oxford. Mid-late sixteenth century.**

Fig. 43. Moulded Rhenish stoneware *Schnelle*, made in Siegburg, Germany with an inscription 'Judit ano 1572'. Judith is shown holding the head of Holfernes, whom she had murdered to save her people. Old Angel Inn 1883.49. (Ht. 20 cm. incomplete).

It is clear that German craftsmen were being inspired by the cultural revival of classical antiquity in all its forms during the second half of the sixteenth century, whose impulse came from Italy. German potters rapidly absorbed this new learning and the acanthus leaf decoration in particular shows the assimilation of antique design. Some pots had pious inscriptions, '[Wer] drinck und est goddes neit vergeist' (Drink and Eat but forget not God) or 'Drinck und est, under der armen nit verges' (Drink and eat and do not forget the poor), which are similar in sentiment to contemporary English inscriptions found in Elizabethan interiors and later adopted by the slipware potters working in Stuart England. The lettering on such pots is often mispelt or applied upside down: Marc Solon, a French craftsman potter, working in England at Mintons (the important ceramic manufacturers) suggests in 1883 that the use of lettering as a decorative element is often adopted by cultures where reading is rare. So these Rhenish stonewares may inform us about the skills and influences behind the German craftsmen and the tastes of the consumers and purchasers which they supplied.

Pottery finds indicate that Oxford in the last quarter of the sixteenth century was part of this continental trade, affecting the commercial centre of the town and colleges such as Magdalen. However, few of these styles were found in excavations in the south western suburbs of the town, suggesting that their primary impact was not in the ordinary household of the day.

Seventeenth Century Stuart Oxford

By 1600 the intellectual freedom and the competitive spirit to achieve had been established in England in the renaissance spirit. The early seventeenth century saw the population in Oxford rapidly expanding, and amongst its craftsmen were pewterers and cutlers from elsewhere; Oxford 'knives' became prized nationally. Forks had been introduced slightly earlier. Immigrants came to the city as apprentices, the food and drink trade flourished, the road carriers were busy. Alchemy, the pursuit of gold made from baser metals, and potion-making often depicted in still life paintings in northern Europe, continued to capture popular imagination; Elias Ashmole (founder of the collection) was a student of magic, alchemy and astrology besides having many other interests. Apothecaries shops were often scientific laboratories, and in Catte Street in the heart of the University a domed redware alembic or apothecary's still, glazed glossy brown, glass phials and drug pots were found, including one inscribed 'Nym... (perhaps after Nymphae candida, associated with alchemical practice or an apothecaries shop see Fig. 5, the alembic is not illustrated). Leases dating to the early seventeenth century show practionners in 'physic' to have worked close by or on the place of discovery. Bruce-Mitford rescued eight red earthenware vessels from the New Bodleian site which were believed at the time to be acoustic jars, but early text books on Chemistry published first in France and later in England show these to be associated with distillation practices (Fig. 44). Other vessels found nearby, unique to the Oxford repertoire, are probably associated with distillation practices too.

Masques were a popular form of entertainment of the period, and often satirised daily life. So it was with the jolly *Bartmann* jugs of Ben Jonson's day: 'Justice Jug's daughter' ran away with a kinsman, her father pursued her and when they caught sight of one another 'they were both, for the time, turn'd to stone', until 'a jug of the town-ale reconciling them the memorial of both their gravities, his in beard and hers in belly, hath remained ever since preserved in picture upon most stone jugs of the Kingdom'.

In spite of a certain intellectual freedom; superstitions still had a place: witchcraft had been an obsession during the fifteenth and sixteenth centuries, and

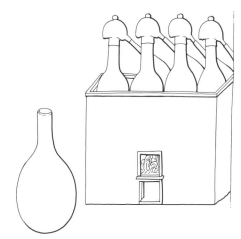

Fig. 44. Distillation vessels in a furnace after an illustration from a chemical textbook. Eight similar wheel-thrown red earthenware vessels came from the New Bodleian site – opposite the Old Ashmolean building, where Plot set up the first chemical laboratory. One excavated vessel displayed a batch mark (detail right). Mid to late seventeenth century. New Bodleian 1937.400. (Ht. 35 cm.).

Fig. 45. Wheel-thrown redwares glazed orange or brown. A local production centre had added large storage jars to their repertoire, also Dutch inspired tripod pipkins and chamber pots. Early-mid seventeenth century.

by the seventeenth century ceramic 'witches bottles' containing brass pins, iron nails, heart-shaped pieces of felt and urine were perceived as a good remedy for the victim (for type of vessel associated with 'witches bottles' see Fig. 48).

The increase in literacy and cheaper printing and engraving helped ideas to spread; and the citizens of Oxford were able to embrace new fashions brought to this country by continental craftsmen. Tin-glazed earthenware tankards copying contemporary pewter or silver shapes were recovered from the Radcliffe Camera and the New Bodleian excavations in the heart of the University (see Earthenware in the Collection). These products would increase in popularity: some were continental in origin, others from London, but all were probably brought to Oxford by barge and their European roots lie with Renaissance Italy and Spain. The city at least continued to reflect an economic upturn.

The medieval tradition of making pots continued in the countryside at Brill until the second quarter of the seventeenth century, it was then rapidly replaced by redwares of the post-medieval period. These redwares were fired at a much higher temperature than the medieval tradition and some major changes in firing technology must have occurred. As yet too little is known to understand the processes behind this change. Was it stimulated by Flemish craftsmen or potters from further north? The redwares are not well represented in the collection, although sooted tripod pipkins, platters, dishes, bowls, pans, crocks, pancheons and chamber pots of this period were excavated in Oxford's south west quarter of St. Ebbe's. Tripod pipkins and chamber pots are introduced from the Low Countries; these had been fashionable in their own country in the fourteenth century, but were not commonplace in this country until the mid seventeenth century (Fig. 45).

The shift towards storage and preserving in jars with wide mouths, begun in the sixteenth century, is continued by the redware industry. Abingdon and Culham to the south of Oxford were exporting apples and butter in ceramic pots, presumably redwares, down-river at this time.

Fig. 46. Wheel-thrown and moulded English and Continental wares from the Fleur-de-Luce, discarded in a cess-pit at the back of the premises. Left back: an Anglo-Netherlandish dish with hand-painted blue marks on the reverse. In the foreground a north Italian Ligurian tin-glaze bowl (one of two) and a unique Rhenish stoneware flagon with Renaissance style friezes around the neck (right). Ligurian products are almost unknown from excavations away from ports in this country.

Fig. 47. Wheel-thrown cooking and serving vessels from the Surrey/Hampshire Border industry; blackwares from the Midlands formed part of an assemblage possibly used by the principal of Hart Hall or his family. Mid seventeenth century.

Pottery production must have been affected at Brill during the years of the Civil War (1642-1645), for the hill-top village played a spirited part. The call by the Royalists in Oxford that all metal be melted down for armaments should have been an economic blessing for the local potters, but this shortfall may have been met by the Surrey/Hampshire border potters. Border wares were supplied to the courts in London and Hampton Court and may well have continued to supply the Royalists when they made Oxford their headquarters (1642-1646). Certainly the pottery population in Oxford assemblages did increase at this time and whitewares from the Surrey/Hampshire border with a wide range of serving dishes appear to have ousted redwares in popularity for a short period.

One of the largest mid seventeenth-century assemblages was recovered from the city ditch at the Bodleian Tunnel (see Part II), and the ditch was clearly a repository for domestic rubbish during or immediately after the Civil War. Few pots were complete but they infill what is still a weak period in the City's ceramic chronology, notably the mid seventeenth century, pre-dating the Sheldonian Theatre of 1664-9. Another fragment of a ceramic distillation

vessel from this area together with the vessels already mentioned may suggest that this area of Oxford concentrated on scientific or 'industrial' practises during the seventeenth century.

The most impressive assemblage of this period however was found to the rear of the Fleur-de-Luce inn (117-119 St Aldates). The property was leased by Anthony Wood's family and the rubbish included local glazed redware drinking vessels, Border wares for cooking and for serving at table: tripod pipkins and a frying pan. Amongst the continental vessels were Italian tin-glaze earthenwares: a small bowl with overall pale blue glaze decorated with dark blue vine leaves and interlocking arcs on the reverse and a small fragmentary dish with similar colouring and decoration on the reverse but with a simple foliate design around the edge of the dish and a rosette in the centre. These are the only known vessels from the Ligurian/Venice production centres in Italy excavated in Oxford and probably date to the late sixteenth century. The lattice design on both vessels favours the Ligurian production centre. Italianate glass drinking vessels were found at the same period associated with Hart Hall. An Anglo-Netherlandish polychrome dish

Fig. 48. **Wheel-thrown Rhenish salt-glaze stonewares with sprig moulded masks and a variety of devices from a pit in the garden of No. 47 Broad Street; one handle with drilled holes was designed to take a metal lid attachment. Such *Bartmann* jugs are sometimes called 'witches bottles'. Late seventeenth century. (Ht. 22.5 cm.; 21.5 cm.; 15 cm.; 21 cm.).**

designed to hang on the wall is also unparalleled locally (Fig. 46, with a chalice and 'patten' on the reverse, hand painted in blue under a colourless lead glaze). Amongst

the Rhenish stonewares was a magnificent example of a wheel-thrown flagon with 'cut glass' decoration and cobalt blue colouring and a Renaissance style frieze around the neck (Fig. 46), suggesting the Wood family had some wealthy connections. The flagon is difficult to provenance within the Rhenish production centres and its shape together with the decorative motifs is new to their repertoire.

By the middle of the seventeenth century Oxford was ranked 'eighth among English provincial towns' and the population had trebled since the mid sixteenth century. Market gardeners, tennis-court keepers, earthenware dealers are recorded, also tobacco pipe-makers. Clay pipes were a novelty at this period and some dating to the 1640s-1670s were recovered from the King Edward Street development (see Part II);

other early examples were recorded from the excavations for the underground bookstore on the north side at the Radcliffe Camera.

Bruce-Mitford was able to marry some of the below-ground archaeology of the site of the New Bodleian with the documentary evidence when he identified the rubbish associated with Hart Hall. This assemblage included a porringer identical to that found with a hoard of coins believed to be deposited *c.*1640 AD at Childrey Manor to the south of Oxford. The Oxford assemblage was dominated by Border ware from the south with very few redwares, and also some fragmentary yellow earthenware slipwares and tin-glaze earthenware that are not illustrated (Fig. 47).

It was usual to send out to the taverns for wine, this practise may explain why numerous bottles with tavern signs are found at sites of eating houses or inns. An example is in King Edward Street, where vintner's stamps include The Three Tuns with a vintner's bush above three tuns and the initials H. B. for Humphrey Bodicote who held one of the five taverns in the City until 1666. The Three Tuns was a short walk away under the northern end of what is now University College; 'The Mermaid', earlier 'The Swyndlestock' (on the south west corner of Carfax) with a bottle stamped '1686' when Anthony Hall was the licensee; a similar range of bottle stamps from seventeenth century taverns were rescued by Bruce-Mitford at the New Bodleian. Coffee house keepers appear for the first time too. Pottery was now sold through retail outlets, (chandlers, mercers and grocers) as well as through market stalls and hawkers.

The University emerged at this time with renewed intellectual energy, and a buoyant economy resulted in the building of the magnificent architectural edifices which were the work-places of Plot, Wood, and their scientist colleagues (see Methods of Manufacture earlier). Oxford was now the scientific centre of the nation and the study of antiquities re-emerged. More information about individuals and their crafts are recorded; diaries began to be kept, potters recipes jotted down so that we can place the ceramics in the wider historical record.

Staffordshire relief-decorated dishes ornamented with symbols of life, were found in King Edward Street. These appealed to popular taste, as did the black glazed vessels including tygs (cups with more than one handle glazed with iron-rich glaze) which were to become very popular across the Midlands. Examples from the commercial centre and the University area are represented in the collection, but excavations in the south-west of Oxford have produced relatively few such vessels. Smaller amounts from Staffordshire were sold by the potter to the 'Cratemen' for distribution, Plot records the 'poor *Crate-men*, who carry them [the pots] at their *backs* all over the Country'; these hawkers from the north Midlands later came by packhorse.

It may have been the local slipware industries centred on Brill and Potterspury which ensured that Staffordshire Slipwares never achieved a more substantial foothold in Oxford. King Edward Street also boasted the widest range of Anglo-Netherlandish tin-glaze earthenwares in the City, some of which may be associated with the retail outlet of James Pen (Fig. 86 and see Part II A Portrait of Evans and Inferences for Oxford's Post-Medieval Heritage).

New drinking habits spurred on new designs of vessel. Coffee was introduced from the Levant, with the first coffee house forming part of the Old Angel Inn (see Part II), later tea from the Orient and chocolate; they were a gift to English potters, inspiring a new range of drinking vessels. Flatwares, designed either for display or to carry food to table, included the great slipware dishes of Thomas Toft, with loyal images in support of the Stuart line of royal succession. The dining room, a new concept of the period, was increasingly important; the domestic conditions for some, at least were improving (see display).

In the later seventeenth century brewing was still very important in Oxford economic life, both University and town being prodigious consumers of beer, ale and wine. College manciples (housekeepers) regularly spent large sums of money on beer for their colleges and many had second jobs related to the provisioning trades. Many inn-keepers were also college cooks and butlers; several cooks lived in the vicinity of the New Bodleian and Radcliffe Camera Excavations (see Part II) and their rubbish forms part of the seventeenth and

Fig. 49. **Wheel-thrown vessels, whitewares glazed yellow or green: innovations for the table, the knobbed chafing dish, heating stands and the four-legged stew pot inspired by Dutch and German prototypes. Heating stands and bird whistles, sometimes used as bird lures, are rare in Oxford assemblages. The stewpot was thrown on a wheel and the lid was then cut out of the side. Recognisable chamber pots are present from the mid seventeenth century onwards. Late seventeenth century.**

eighteenth-century collection. Bottles from Normandy, discarded mainly in the University area, may have contained calvedos (Fig. 59).

The later *Bartmann* jugs, more formalised with fake heraldic styles, narrower at the top and bottom than earlier vessels, were meeting increasing competition from glass bottles, and this finally led to the eclipse of the imported bottle (Fig. 48).

These Rhenish wares had stimulated native production and English salt-glazed stoneware industry was born (see Dwight earlier). The Rhenish trade persisted, however, with the introduction of Westerwald tankards and jugs from the Rhineland, which became increasingly popular at the very end of the seventeenth century (Fig. 50).

Other innovations for the household included bed pans and warming pans. A contemporary description describes the warming pan's use: 'to receive either hot coales, or an iron heater in to it, which being shut closse with a cou[v]er for the purpose, the maide warmes her maisters Bed'.

Local redwares copied earlier seventeenth-century Border ware shapes — the porringer with horizontal loop handle and Rhenish stoneware shapes suggest a certain sentimentality for a past epoch. The Surrey/ Hampshire production centres have many similarities with the German whiteware industry at this period and new shapes for cookery were introduced from the Continent: a four-legged stew-pot, possibly from the Rhineland is an example. This type of stewpot in the Low Countries is known as a 'pig-pot' possibly because the shape was inspired by bloated pig skins used for storage of liquids, such pig skins are often depicted in misericords in this country. Other new innovations included a Border ware chafing dish and heating stand for keeping food warm at table (Fig. 49).

Formal gardens were in vogue nationally, locally market gardening was a growing industry and flowers in ceramic vases and in garden pots were a re-occurring theme in paintings of the period and on Dutch tin-glaze tiles. A late seventeenth-century household inventory in Abingdon, a market town to the south of Oxford, mentions 'flower potts' and 'earthenware pots holding soil'. There are no obvious ceramic flower pots amongst the Ashmolean collection, but a lead glazed earthenware rose type watering pot found in an 'ancient well' behind the Randolph Hotel, on the site of Oxenford Hall presents tangible evidence of gardening in Stuart Oxford. The design had evolved from the medieval sprinkler (Fig. 41) to one with a rose for dispensing water, similar to the present day galvanised steel or plastic watering cans.

It is during the seventeenth century that ceramics in the collection give us the greatest insight into the changing lifestyles of Oxford inhabitants, the social and economic history of the period. The social and functional differentiation between some households is more marked than in the medieval period. Despite some bias in collecting, the University area appears to have invested in more tin-glaze earthenware pharmaceutical pots. Communal eating houses preferred plain stonewares and large serving dishes, and a greater variety of stonewares appear associated with the commercial centre than in the excavated suburbs. Scientific investigation had led to increased technical skills, culminating in a wider range of pottery types catering for the domestic household, communal eating houses and industrial uses, as well as leisure pursuits such as gardening. Taverns and communal eating houses had increased, resulting in an explosion in ceramic trade, most of which was no longer of local manufacture. The non local pottery may have been transported either by barge or by packhorse. In the 1690s Siberechts, a Flemish landscape painter, painted a topographical scene in south east Oxfordshire entitled 'Henley on Thames', which included barges on the river Thames and packhorses trudging along the road towards east Berkshire and Surrey — a route which could have led to the Border ware production centres.

Travel was now more commonplace, either by water or through the introduction of coaching, and both Anthony Wood and Elias Ashmole travelled to and from London by coach. More time was devoted to sport and pastimes, as illustrated by Manning's lectures (see Part II).

This change in social mobility and structure is mirrored in the towns and cities across England, but in the rural areas the change was less marked, and this is reflected in the pottery types in use, where redwares still dominated. In the urban areas the ceramic products were no longer tied to the traditional medieval colours of greens and reddish browns but now embraced the whole spectrum. These visually stimulating ceramic products were to become the material symbols of wealth and power in the early eighteenth century, but their ornamentation owes much to the European Renaissance and to the contemporary entrepreneurs who encouraged the producers to supply and the consumers to buy decorative wares.

Fig. 50. Decorated tin-glaze plate, bowls and teawares copying porcelain shapes (the base and the bowl of the same vessel were recovered in 1911 and 1915 and only recently found to join); colourful Rhenish stoneware drinking jugs and tankards, pre-date 1737, reflecting the taste of the period. Jackson Collection.

Eighteenth Century Georgian Oxford

The new wealth at the beginning of the century saw the continued growth in ceramic products, in particular the straight sided 'ale-mugs', manufactured in London, such as those from the Leopold Arms (the Bocardo) and the coaching inn: the Old Angel Inn (see Part II). The introduction of stamped excise marks on these tavern mugs, 'WR' and 'AR' became the hall-mark of all early eighteenth-century mugs, and indicates a tightening of standards by the victual trade (Figs 51 and 89). 'AR' excise marks were rare on mugs excavated in Oxford's south west quarter of St. Ebbe's and the fine Staffordshire style stonewares only occur in the University area.

The collection from the area of the new Masonic Hall in the High Street included some fine late sixteenth century *Bartmann* jugs with flowing beards and legends; other artefacts besides those illustrated (Fig. 51) included a glass seal stamped 'Chas. Turner 1690', a Mr. Turner, vintner, lived in a house in St Mary's Entry about 1710 and a fragment of an English stoneware ale mug bearing the arms of the University.

Drinking and tavern life was still to the fore in this market and university city, but coffee houses were more popular and the laying down of wine by the colleges saw the demise of the tavern at the end of the century. The quality of the beer was not all it should have been however. In 1729 the keeper of the Ashmolean Museum died after drinking 'a pretty deal of bad small beer' supplied by Christ Church. In 1756 Samuel Johnson, the author, wit and 'shameless tea-drinker' was to return to Oxford to the famous Bodleian Library and saw the Radcliffe Camera in all its new glory. The teapots that Johnson 'bequeathed' to his College remain in the care of Pembroke college, to this day.

The major change in the heart of the University at the Radcliffe Camera site provides an excellent end date of 1737; the properties purchased were cleared away and their below-ground deposits sealed. The material collected by Jackson from this site is the best in the City for ornamented Westerwald stonewares and tin-glaze earthenware bowls; the tin-glaze bowls were decorated with fine blue brushwork, imitating Chinese porcelain (Fig. 50). The occasional stoneware coffee pots, imitating Queen Anne silver, make a fitting appearance for the first time in the city on the Radcliffe Camera site, for Dr Radcliffe had been physician to Queen Anne. Together with the Staf-

45

Fig. 51. Wheel-thrown black glazed drinking vessels; moulded slipware and a salt-glazed stoneware tea pot from the north Midlands were collected with glass sack bottles dated '1713' and '1715' respectively and a glass seal 'Chas. Turner 1690'. Stoneware drinking tankards with moulded 'A.R.' ciphers and cobalt blue decoration were also contemporary and were discarded with chamber pots in the area later built over for the new Masonic Hall. Early-mid eighteenth century.

Metropolitan wares of London and the south Midlands (which in turn mirrored the Flemish and north German tradition) were made at Brill in the seventeenth and eighteenth centuries. Large Brill red earthenware slipware platters used as communal serving dishes as rescued from the Leopold Arms site (Bocardo see Part II, Fig. 89) and the Radcliffe Camera, and red earthenware chamber pots decorated internally were the most popular eighteenth century products.

Two slipware dishes originating from either Staffordshire or Bristol with combed decoration, were found to have moulded relief initials at the centre 'PM' and 'IP'. Another marked dish with initial 'M' was recovered from the excavations in the south west of Oxford.

Dinnerwares however are entirely absent from the Radcliffe Camera site with the exception of a few tin-glaze earthenware plates, and their absence may be of chronological significance. The *terminus ante quem* of 1737 on this site probably means that the press-moulded Staffordshire white salt-glaze dinner plates and dinner plates from other production centres were not available to Oxford citizens until the middle of the century, when mass production was just beginning to be recognised as the only way to make business viable (see Brolliet in Methods of Manufacture).

The Staffordshire potteries came to dominate the second half of the eighteenth century and were supplying markets throughout the world. The demand for these wares in Oxford, quickly gained momentum, and 'China dealers' are recorded at two venues in the University area. Some colleges began to mark their crockery in the same way as they had identified their earlier stoneware mugs, a practise adopted by the colleges in Cambridge too. There are however no collections for this period in the Antiquities department.

Redwares continued to be in demand in the countryside and the eighteenth century saw a great increase in country potters; almost every large village had a pothouse, supplying the needs of local and rural communities. Large lidded vessels, big pans, bread crocks, milk skimmers, colanders, vegetable dishes and flower pots were added to the repertoire. In the city redwares were less common, but chamber pots and later paint pots, bowls and large pitchers remained in demand.

Oxford boasted some twenty coffee houses, patronised largely by the University, at the end of

fordshire type slipwares (see Fig. 14), Chinese porcelain (Fig. 12) and tin-glaze earthenwares (teawares of the eighteenth century including bowls, shallow dishes or saucers), these ceramics suggest the owners or occupiers enjoyed a level of prosperity wholly consistent with the material symbols of wealth of the eighteenth century, rather than the inmates of a 'a huddle of old houses'. Local slipwares copying the

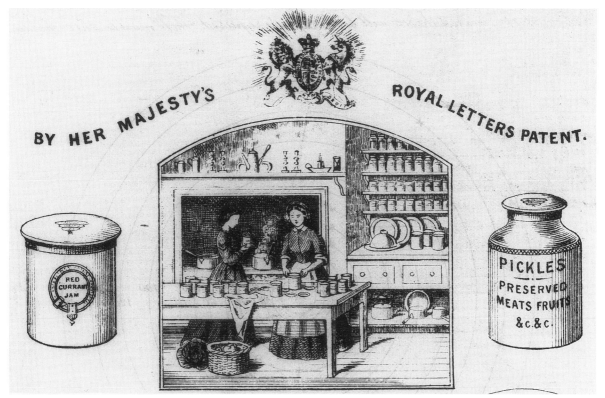

Fig. 52. An engraving of the interior of a nineteenth century kitchen with white earthenware jars – the cylindrical shapes were adopted by Cooper's Oxford Marmalade, originally made on part of the site of the Old Angel Inn. Courtesy of Bodleian Library.

the century. White earthenwares and printed pottery graced their interiors and replaced the English stonewares.

Nineteenth Century Victorian Oxford

Oxford was still very rural in aspect at the beginning of the nineteenth century. The 1790s saw the completion of the canal opening up a new highway from the north Midlands to Oxford. Mass-produced wares from the Staffordshire potteries continued to saturate the market (Fig. 52). From the corner of St. Aldates and Queen Street (Glyn Mills Bank), once the site of The Mermaid and earlier the Swyndlestock (see Fourteenth/Fifteenth Century earlier and Part II), a group of early nineteenth-century fine press-moulded and slip-cast wares was rescued. The pearlwares, developed by Josiah Wedgewood, an innovation of *c.*1780s when cobalt blue was added to the lead glaze over a modified cream earthenware, dominated the group. This earthenware was an ideal background for blue hand-painted and blue transfer-printed decoration, with its *floruit* in the early-mid nineteenth century.

Products included a pepper-pot copying a silver shape, cylindrical tankards and bowls, hand-painted jars and jugs, and flatwares with transfer-printed engravings. A cylindrical jug, with hand-painted decoration with the initials E, G OX in yellow on a brown background, was clearly commissioned for someone in Oxford. This is the latest archaeological assemblage in the museum's collection (Fig. 92).

The Brill and Leafield potteries continued their traditional craft, specialising in redwares. Manning collected two lamp-stands made by Thomas Hubbocks of Brill in 1861; this part of Manning's collection is now on loan to the Buckinghamshire County Museum. Some country potters started to seek inspiration from earlier periods, and examples are evident at the Leafield Potteries where Manning purchased a delightful money box with a cuckoo perched on the knob, a shape dating back to the fifteenth century (Fig. 53).

Manning also collected redwares from the corner of Cornmarket/Broad Street in 1914 these included a chick feeder, one of three from central Oxford sites. Some other innovations were introduced, giving an insight into the changing social history of the time:

Fig. 53. Wheel-thrown redwares made by the Franklin family in Leafield, north west Oxfordshire: honey pot, jug inscribed 'W. Simms 1898', tobacco jar with rusticated decoration and a money box with cuckoo finial. Late nineteenth century. Manning Collection. Leafield 1921.244, 241, 246 and 243. (Ht. 9.8 cm.; 16.5 cm.; 13.4 cm.; 13 cm.). Courtesy of Oxfordshire Museums Service.

wall pendant baskets and tobacco jars such as those made by the Franklin family of Leafield were widely adopted and found in almost every rural home, indicating an increasing interest in material goods which were now affordable by a wider group of people.

The ceramic stylistic developments and technical innovations throughout this long temporal span, from the ninth to nineteenth centuries, have several stories to tell. They show periods of continuity and stability: the conservatism of some traditions, the diffusion of others; other periods of change: the rapid fluctuations in decorative designs and technology; the paucity of assemblages of the fifteenth and sixteenth centuries; the social and functional differentiation between discreet areas of the town, be they University, commercial or suburban; movements in distribution and

trade: local, regional and continental economic links and their political implications. All these aspects, contribute to a picture of the past, while the collection fulfills its primary purpose of the 'provision of material essential for the teaching of students of history, archaeology and art'.

What more can we learn from these pots?

Pottery vessels had a very wide range of uses. Paintings, manuscript illustrations, sculpture and tapestrys sometimes depict pottery. Written records such as recipes (culinary, medicinal and industrial), account books, books of etiquette and household inventories often mention a variety of ceramic vessels in use. Some pots were merely containers for dried foodstuffs, malt or honey — prior to the Norman Conquest, Oxford regularly paid the king in honey for tolls, tribute and other dues.

The residual contents in the vessel can indicate the type of foodstuffs eaten and the beverages consumed, be they ale or wine or the ointments used. Anthony Wood, the seventeenth century antiquarian, recounts a tradition at Merton College, Oxford, on Shrove Tuesday. A freshman had to give a speech, and if it went well the freshman received a 'cup of cawdle'. 'If indifferent, some cawdle and some falted drink; but if dull, nothing was given to him but falted drink, or salt put in the college beere, with tucks to boot'. Cawdle was dispensed in ceramic or silver posset pots and passed round from guest to guest (Fig. 54).

Jugs in the collection often display thick deposits of calcium carbonate internally, suggesting they were habitually used for heating water, and their bases are also sooted. Similar white encrustations may result after the evaporation of urine: urine was widely used in diagnostic medicine and also in industrial processes such as tanning.

The associated sooting patterns apparent on plain household vessels and the decorated jugs in the collection may indicate the method of heating employed (see Figs. 3 and 32, top shelf). The magnificent Bayeux tapestry shows several methods of cooking employed during the eleventh-twelfth century. Chaucer in *Canterbury Tales* tells how fourteenth century cooks 'could roast and fry and boil and stew, make dainty pottage and bake pies well' and this is confirmed by a contemporary illuminated manuscript (Fig. 55). Such complete vessels can inform the archaeologist how the vessels were used.

Archaeo-botanical evidence has enormous potential: germinating barley and hops have been found in

Fig. 54. Tin-glaze earthenware posset pot, hand-painted in dark blue in the Renaissance style with initials 'E. M.' dated 1653. Unprovenanced 1986.21. (Ht. 10 cm.).

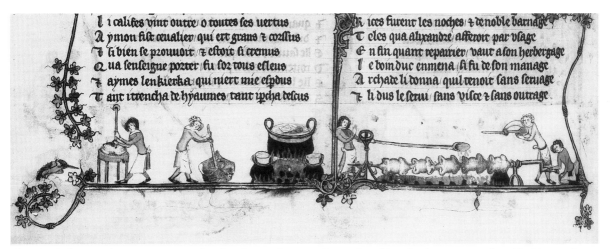

Fig. 55. A fourteenth century manuscript showing cooks preparing and cooking food; pots were placed inside metal cauldrons along with other ingredients for a meal; long handled wooden spoons were used to baste the meat cooking on the spit. From *The Romance of Alexander*. Courtesy of Bodleian Library.

association with ceramic bung-hole jars in Norwich (Norfolk) at the end of the medieval period when there was a gradual change from ale to beer. Some citizens enjoyed a rich diet of exotic fruits, the Provost of Oriel College, Oxford in the mid seventeenth century ate some ten species of fruit including redcurrants, figs, mulberries, walnuts, plums, grapes, raspberries and these were discarded with tin-glaze earthenwares and a Chinese porcelain dish.

Ceramic vessels were used in industrial processes too, precious metals were melted in crucibles in the workshop or laboratory (Fig. 26); Plot specified the use of 'new earthenpots, well glazed' to ensure reproducable results from his scientific experiments.

Pots were ubiquitious and were included in children's games and pastimes (Fig. 56). Novelties were introduced into the potter's repertoire, such as bird whistles which were as popular in continental Europe, as in this country and which continue to be made even today, albeit in plastic! While up at Oxford Samuel Johnson, a reluctant undergraduate, at Pembroke College, chased a *servitor* (a poor scholar who waited at table) with a candlestick clattering in a chamber pot. The noise of this empty vessel was clearly intimidating, and ceramic vessels could on occasions also be used as weapons, as witnessed at the St Scholastica's Day riot (Fig. 35) and in the Flemish still life paintings of the seventeenth century.

More rarely pots were installed in chancels in churches in Britain to improve the acoustics. Not infrequently vessels were buried beneath the foundations of new buildings to bring good fortune, a custom continued to this day (see Part II Fig. 83). Birdpots were

attached beneath the eaves of houses to encourage nesting in the Low Countries, as illustrated in sixteenth and seventeenth century engravings in the Douce collection (see Part II under Jackson). Individual pots were collected for themselves, as now, as personal souvenirs of a pilgrimage or a visit, or because they were merely visually attractive. By the mid

Fig. 56. Pots were used in pastimes, as depicted in this manuscript where a child is blindfolded and holds a 'bat'. Such pots might be discarded far from their primary place of disposition, causing havoc to any archaeological interpretation! Courtesy of Bodleian Library.

fourteenth century pilgrimages had become an enormous industry, and Oxford was an important centre, continued to this day, although for more secular than religious reasons.

In archaeological study complete vessels or profiles are used to build up information on shape and form, leading to a typology, a progressive development of a specific shape (Fig. 57). The baluster jugs from the Brill/Boarstall production centre are quite distinct from those of Nottingham or London. Such vessels could be systematically measured to establish their capacity, which might give an insight into the local food trades and associated laws concerned with price, measure, quality and competition. Shapes and capacity are also important when determining function.

The evolution of the potter's craft and associated iconography can indicate technological and stylistic influences, developments and achievements as portrayed by the decorative schemes on the Rhensh stoneware, which reflect the life of the people involved. They may also be compared with other contemporary traditional crafts, by art historians and archaeologists, to give a wider perspective on medieval life. Wood, metal, wicker and glass all played their part and competed with ceramic pots — but survive less well in the archaeological record than ceramics.

The chronological framework used to build up a more complete picture of Oxford's past is based on stratified sequences from controlled excavations over the past thirty years, building on the work of earlier archaeologists (see Part II for Bruce-Mitford and see earlier Methods of Manufacture for Jope and Part II). The sequences reveal trends and patterns in pottery production over long periods. The variations in local

Fig. 58. Hand-modelled earthenware figurine on a tubular spouted pitcher, reminiscent of the monkeys illustrated in the margins of illuminated manuscripts of the period. Thirteenth century. Exeter College 1984.1075. (Ht. 11 cm.).

clay, vessel shapes and glaze technology are so marked that the source of many of the ceramic vessels is now readily identifiable.

Scientific analysis such as archaeomagnetism (used by physicists to determine the date at which a vessel was fired), dendrochronology and radio-carbon dating have all enhanced these traditional techniques. The skill and expertise of the numismatists has continued to tighten this chronology. The potential of ceramic research is growing as scientific techniques improve and as new methods of analysis are developed and adapted by archaeologists and by those working in related disciplines.

The whole or near complete vessels in the medieval and later collection of the Ashmolean have been set in this new framework, and can now be studied to indicate their social and economic differentiation (as seen in the previous section). Pottery in the medieval and later period is a product used by all levels of society and the ceramic traditions and styles vary regionally. It is the creation of the potter craftsman/artisan, and it must reflect also the beliefs and values of the society and culture in which it was produced. The skilfully decorated anthropomorphic jugs with faces and arms, for example, portray the spirit and robust humour of the potter, and presumably the tastes of the patron or commissioning purchaser.

Medieval humour probably differs little from that of twentieth century man: personality, taste, and the surrounding environment are all contributory factors to the final product (Fig. 58).

These pots are also a commodity and can be used to study and illuminate aspects of trade and exchange networks. Ceramic containers with oil, ginger, and sugar were brought on Catalan, Basque and Italian

Fig. 57. A typology of baluster type jugs from the Brill/Boarstall workshops. These tall slender vessels were the most popular jug shape throughout the Middle Ages. Mid thirteenth-fifteenth century.

ships. Wine was imported in quantity from France and Rhineland from as early as the eleventh century. Empty vessels, probably covered in wicker, designed for transport, found their way inland away from the ports in the seventeenth century (Fig. 59).

The quantity, quality, the range and capacity of vessels present, can give an insight into the status and wealth of the consumers, or of the traders who stocked such vessels. Much complimentary information of this kind was recovered by the Revd. Herbert Salter, who researched the medieval documents from the City of Oxford and related certain tenements to individual occupiers, so highlighting the purposes for which the buildings were used.

The goods available, notably from mercers' or grocers' shops, are sometimes documented in probate inventories of the late sixteenth and seventeenth centuries (see earlier). The prices for probate do not necessarily reflect market prices, but are nevertheless invaluable to the ceramic historian for comparative studies.

The potential of ceramic research continues to grow as new methods of analysis are developed. 'Archaeology is about discovery', in the search for a better understanding of the human past and of everyday life. Pottery is a vital component of archae-ology: available in statistically significant quantities, unravelling the changes in taste, teasing out the human background behind the pots, plotting market trends and distribution networks, which may be underpinned by the exchange of other artefacts or trade. Once discarded, the sherds of pottery can help date structures and sequences to anchor a site in time and context more securely.

The relative size of fragments, the wear, abrasion and dispersal of the sherds across a site may give valuable information as to how the vessels were dispersed. The development of a specific site and any subsequent soil movement can be established through the careful study of ceramics. These are just some of the questions that can be addressed from research, founded on the principles of medieval ceramics in archaeology.

We have considered the craftsmen potter and the artisan at the production centre, and the patron and consumer in the town and rural countryside but what of the collectors? Without their vision and energy in the second half of the nineteenth and early twentieth century our knowledge of medieval and later ceramic forms and shapes would have been greatly impoverished.

Fig. 59. Imported wheel-thrown earthenwares: Normandy bottles originally with earthen stoppers; a Spanish/ Portuguese two handled costrel and a water carrier, the latter often depicted in Spanish paintings by Murillo (1618-1682) and Velasquez (1599-1660); northern French: Martincamp-type flasks. Seventeenth century.

Part II:
Genesis of the Collection

The public collection as displayed is combined from private collections of individual Victorian, Edwardian and later fieldworkers.

The early lives of some of these pioneers may hold the key to why successive generations of enthusiasts were intrigued by the ceramics which form the collections that we enjoy today. Why are some people collectors, what inspires them to acquire objects and how do they develop such an appreciation, what kindles their interest?

— PORTRAIT —

Keeper of Ashmole's Collection: Dr Robert Plot

Dr Robert Plot of Magdalen Hall (1640–96), a scholar of remarkable energy, was the first keeper of the Ashmolean Museum (1683–1690), the oldest public museum in Britain (Fig. 60). He represented a continuum of the ideals of the Renaissance which emphasised the potential of the individual and this life.

Fig. 61. An engraving after T. Wood by Michael Burghers 1685 of The Old Ashmolean, a Restoration building in the style of a Renaissance palazzio. Wood, the architect, had a tennis court nearby (see Fig. 91). Courtesy of the Museum of the History of Science.

He was working in the handsome Old Ashmolean building (now housing the Museum of the History of Science Fig. 61), at a time widely regarded as the Golden Age of intellectual endeavour of the University, when Restoration scientists rubbed shoulders with local antiquarians and the great architects of the day, many of whom were men of multiple talents. The building of the nearby University library, the Bodleian was nearing completion, and other institutions such as Wren's ingenious Sheldonian Theatre and the Botanical Gardens (sometimes known as the Physic Garden, the oldest in Britain) were founded.

Prior to Plot's appointment to the Ashmolean, he had completed his survey of Oxfordshire. The survey, already under-way by 1674, was undertaken, so Plot said, for his own pleasure. Printed questionnaires designed to secure first-hand information were circulated, and a thorough programme of field-work ensued. After his appointment to the Ashmolean, Plot set about cataloguing the first inventory of Elias Ashmole's foundation collection — twenty six big boxes which eventually arrived by barge from London to Oxford.

The catalogue, in Latin (1685), gives a very complete picture of the foundation collection at that date, with expansive descriptions, reflecting Plot's belief in the necessity of objective observation: 'three earthenware vessels with swelling bodies' are the two Roman pots and an Anglo-Saxon burial urn dated to the fifth

Fig. 60. Portrait of Dr. Plot of Magdalen Hall, the first custodian of the Old Ashmolean Museum and author of the *The Natural History of Oxford-shire* and *The Natural History of Stafford-shire*. Courtesy of the Museum of the History of Science (Old Ashmolean Series 53).

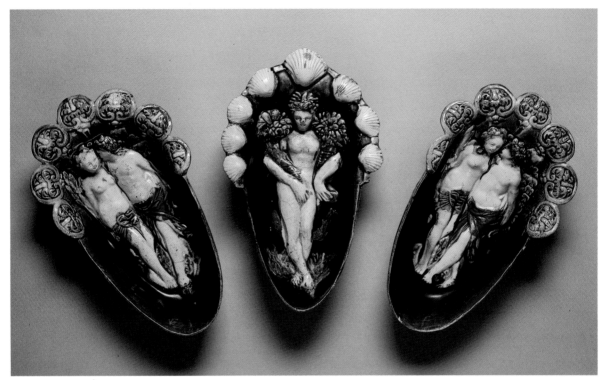

Fig. 62. Press-moulded polychrome-painted earthenware dishes after the style of Palissy, a French potter working *c.*1539-91. Palissy is remembered for his experimental coloured glazes. Early seventeenth century. Tradescant Collection. Mus. Trad. 1685 Cat. B585, B586 and B584. (Ht. 5 cm.).

or sixth century AD (see Part I Fig. 21). Ashmole's collection did not include any medieval earthenware vessels. A recognisable entry is 'four elongated Chinese dishes, in one part they have recumbent naked women covering their pudenda with their hands', which must be the delightful lead-glazed polychrome-painted earthenware oval moulded dishes, probably made in London, dating to the first half of the seventeenth century (Fig. 62).

The eminent Plot set up the Oxford Philosophical Society, modelled on the Royal Society and counted amongst his colleagues the Hon. Robert Boyle and his assistants Robert Hooke and John Dwight, pioneering scientists of the seventeenth century (see Part I).

Three years after his appointment, Plot recorded and published his observations of another county in his *Natural History of the County of Stafford-shire* (1686). Together with his earlier survey *Natural History of Oxford-shire*, his spirit of enquiry laid the foundations for ceramic research in the county, and his Oxfordshire survey was used by Manning in the 1890s and during the first decade of the twentieth century, and still remains an indispensable source for modern day scholars.

Victorian Collectors

The first major group of medieval and later ceramics which was to form the nucleus of the Ashmolean's collection was added some two hundred years after Plot had taken up his curatorship.

— PORTRAIT —

The First Oxford Field Collector: A. J. Evans

Arthur Evans (1851-1941), son of Sir John Evans, a distinguished antiquary, numismatist and collector, was a schoolboy when he first developed an interest in collecting medieval pottery. At the age of 9, after a school expedition in East Anglia, he wrote home announcing his discoveries.

His father, the scholarly ambience that surrounded the family will have helped to direct his enthusiasm also the staff at the Ashmolean. He was not a great scholar while at school at Harrow but his housemaster judged him 'a boy of powerful original mind'. Later as an undergraduate reading Modern History at Brasenose College, Oxford he had the foresight to rescue and purchase a fascinating collection of medieval and later artefacts from workmen engaged in enjoy giving lectures but on occasions combined archaeology and folklore as in the early 1890's when he gave a presentation on 'The Rollright Stones and their Legendary Lore'.

He was appointed Keeper of the Ashmolean in 1884. Like Plot, he was 'formidable in his energy but also had the private means to deploy it to maximum effect'. J. L. Myres remembered his first sight of Evans and his 'erratic gait and constant gestures'. He was frequently abroad, and when the assistant keeper Edward Evans said to Myres that 'the keeper is somewhere in Bohemia' this might imply Oxford or beyond. Evans and Myres were to develop a lifelong friendship and Myres said 'I owe Evans more than I could ever repay' (see Portrait of Manning later). He remained essentially a collector rather than a professional archaeologist. During the period 1900-1908, he excavated the palace of Knossos in Crete, resigned from the Ashmolean in order to spend more time on the Knossos project, and in 1911 he was knighted. More than anyone else, it was his initiative that was responsible 'for the growth of the Ashmolean to the first rate importance on the archaeological side', making it into the finest museum in England outside national collections.

A decade was to pass before the next major contributor to the collection arrived in Oxford and the fruits of Manning's enthusiasms were not deposited with the Ashmolean until twenty years later.

— PORTRAIT —

The First Archaeological Collector of Medieval Artefacts: P. Manning.

The second major contributor to the collection was Percy Manning (1870-1917). Born near Leeds in Yorkshire he came up to Oxford in 1888. At this time Arthur Evans was building up the Ashmolean as the centre of archaeological study. He may not have been so precocious as Evans, for apart from an emphasis on classical scholarship, there is no evidence that Manning was interested in archaeology while still at school at Clifton College, Bristol (1884-88), (although there was an archaeological branch of the College's Scientific Society at the time). Unlike Evans, Manning was an unsatisfactory student: his single-minded pursuit of objects of local antiquity which embraced the prehistoric, Roman and medieval periods from Oxfordshire, Berkshire and Buckinghamshire, was perhaps too narrow for the University. He suffered from 'extreme aphasia' which affected his mode of speaking and he took little

Fig. 63. Portrait of Arthur Evans just after graduating *c.* 1878, remembered for his restless energy.

laying out King Edward Street. The costs of these purchases were reimbursed by the Ashmolean. The acquisitions were meticulously catalogued and researched by Edward Evans, an under-keeper and 'the uncouth guardian of the Old Building' at the Museum (but no relation. Fig. 64).

A year later, in 1874, Arthur Evans was elected to the Oxford Architectural and Historical Society (to be referred to hereafter as OAHS). His tutor found it remarkable that in his final examinations he wrote nothing later than the twelfth century, perhaps as a result of his first-hand experiences with later medieval artefacts in King Edward Street; none the less, he achieved First Class Honours (Fig. 63).

He was an enthusiastic traveller and enjoyed adventure, discovering archaeological sites at Hallstatt in Austria and also in the Balkans during his undergraduate years. He sketched delightful pictures of local people and their costumes — clearly interested in people as well as ideas. Later his sharp eye committed artefacts to paper with the same zeal.

Evans remained an active member of the OAHS and served intermittently as an officer until 1890, thus keeping in touch with local archaeology. He did not

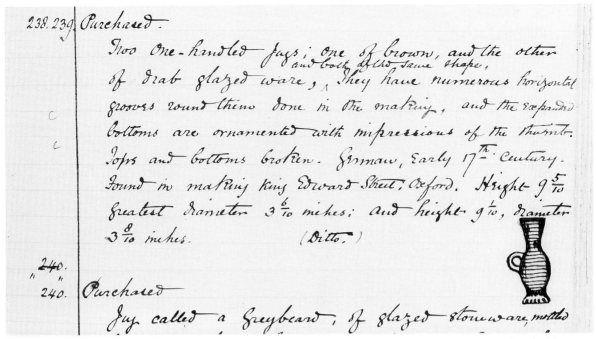

238.239 Purchased.

Two One-handled Jugs; One of brown, and the other and both of the same shape, of drab glazed ware, They have numerous horizontal grooves round them done in the making, and the expanded bottoms are ornamented with impressions of the thumb. Tops and bottoms broken. German, Early 17th. Century. Found in making King Edward Street, Oxford. Height 9 5/10. Greatest diameter 3 6/10 inches; and height 9 1/10, diameter 3 8/10 inches. (Ditto.)

"240.
"240. Purchased
Jug called a Greybeard; of glazed stoneware, mottled

Fig. 64. Original entry from the Museum Accessions Book with a delightful drawing of a Raeren funnel-necked jug, copying a Siegburg shape, glazed grey/brown. Such shapes are depicted in contemporary Continental still life paintings. King Edward Street the vessel 1873.239 cross-joins with 1887.3030.

part in College life, nor did he converse much with the dons, which may have hindered him from obtaining even a pass degree, after five years at New College! His collecting may have been a way of compensating for his speech impediment: a considerable disability in an environment where the scholarly tradition demanded argument and debate.

At university Manning read *Literae Humaniores*, at first concentrating on Greek and Latin literature, and later on ancient history, with a combination of Greek and Latin, with philosophy, both ancient and modern. Classics was perceived as an excellent background for antiquarian pursuits or an archaeological career.

In his first term Manning was elected a member of OAHS, which met in the basement of the Old Ashmolean. During this same term Arthur Evans read a paper to the Society on Stonehenge, illustrating his lecture with large water-colour diagrams. Manning remained an active member of the Society throughout his time in Oxford, along with J. L. Myres. Myres, a direct contemporary of Manning at New College, had joined the Society ten days before Manning. Myres had been an enthusiast of archaeology since a small child when he saw his father's copy of the Quarterly Statement of the Palestine Exploration Fund, showing a picture on the cover of an excavation in progress. Manning and

Myres met through the Society, and later in life Myres records that Manning was already 'a keen field-antiquary'.

These two young men collaborated on local excavations and in 1892 they directed their first excavation at the Roman station at Alcester in north east Oxfordshire, at largely their own expense. Myres was instrumental in thwarting an attempt to send Manning down, when Manning arrived late for Collections, a college internal examination. Manning pleaded 'that the train from Alcester was late' and in the afternoon failed to turn up at all! Myres invited the Dean to visit the excavation at the cross-roads of Akeman street, here the Dean wielded 'a vigorous but untutored pick'. Thereafter the College decided to keep Manning in residence until he finished his work. 'The punishment filled the crime, and was a great relief to Manning'. They both were founder members of the Oxford University Brass Rubbing Society as well as active officers of the OAHS during the 1890's and the first decade of the twentieth century.

In 1891, Manning was elected as Honorary Secretary to the Society, a post he energetically filled until 1898. Manning's first gift to the Ashmolean in 1892, included 'two Roman pots, keys and other articles of iron, mediaeval pottery, a seventeenth century seal

Fig. 65. Portrait of Percy Manning at the Romano-British villa, North Leigh, Oxfordshire *c.* 1910 (dressed as a countryman with numerous pockets in his jacket).

and tradesmen's tokens'. He continued to donate small gifts of artefacts throughout the 1890's, and this must have brought him in contact with both Evans and Charles Bell (see later).

Manning moved out of New College (his name was removed from the College books) and migrated to Marcon's Hall at the end of 1893. 1894 was a particularly auspicious year for Oxford's archaeology. Under his management the Society held a very successful exhibition in the Randolph Hotel, illustrating the objects and interests of the Society. The Randolph (the leading hotel in Oxford built 1863-6) took its name from the Randolph Galleries opposite, and in turn from the Revd. Dr Francis Randolph, whose benefaction to the University in the eighteenth century ultimately provided the finance for the building of the University Galleries, later combined with the Ashmolean.

Fig. 66. Wheel-thrown stoneware utilitarian wares possibly made in Derbyshire *c.*1800. Manning Collection. New Corn Exchange, George Street 1921.231, 230. (Ht. 6.1 cm.; 7.3 cm.).

That same time, i.e. the year of the Randolph Exhibition, under the energetic direction of Arthur Evans the Ashmolean's collection of antiquities moved to its new site, behind the Galleries, and the Ashmolean opened its doors, heralding a new era for archaeological studies.

A catalogue of the 1894 Exhibition shows that Manning was an avid collector of drawings and engravings of the City of Oxford and its county, and this may have brought him to the attention of T. W. Jackson (see later). His topographical prints of the city suggest that he had been collecting over a considerable length of time, although he had only been in Oxford six years. He was clearly a man of independent means, who was able to indulge himself. (His inheritance may have come from his father, who had died when Manning was only three, he was the youngest of four boys). His extensive collection also included encaustic tiles from Oseney Abbey, the largest monastery in Oxford, Rewley Abbey, Godstow Nunnery as well as medieval antiquities found in or connected with the City and University, and he spent much time visiting local churches. Manning also undertook some excavation of the northern end of Oseney Abbey. The restoration of churches in the first half of the nineteenth century and the discarding of medieval tiles led to a renewed interest in those still *in situ*.

At the last meeting of the OAHS in the old museum building Manning exhibited brass rubbings from churches in Yorkshire, presumably undertaken by himself. He continued to be a frequent exhibitor at the Society's meetings from 1895-1906, and on occasions lectured to the Society with a series of lantern slides, despite his supposed speech impediment (Myres had pioneered the use of lantern slides in 1895). In 1899 Manning was elected Vice President of the Society and was assiduous in his attendance at meetings until the onset of World War I. His contribution to local archaeology was such that he was elected a Fellow of the Society of Antiquaries in the mid 1890s, having finally completed his degree.

Interestingly Manning did not initially recover assemblages of whole pots or near complete vessels from any one site as had Evans. He collected, instead individual rare artefacts in the medieval tradition of the exotic or miscellaneous, such as a spiked cresset lamp from the Old Music School in 1892, the utilitarian stoneware drinking vessels from George Street and a very fine tooth and nail brush container, with polychrome decoration, from the 'Angel Hotel, Oxford' (Figs. 66 and 67).

Fig. 67. Moulded polychrome tooth and nail brush box in Mason's ironstone – a durable earthenware. A charming set suitable for use by Royalty. Queen Adelaide, consort of William IV, stayed at the hotel in 1835. Detail: brown crown with the words 'Real Stone China' (67a) dating the piece to post 1822. The inn closed in 1866. The Old Angel Inn 1921.273. (Ht. 6.9 cm.).

Manning's archive held in the Bodleian Library includes maps, plans and prints of many of the early unpublished sites, suggesting that he was familiar with the unpublished collections housed in the Ashmolean Museum. His sketches of tile designs and some twenty five drawings of ceramic vessels show that while not a great draughtsman he could convey sufficient detail to identify the original today. Manning was the first person to 'quietly and persistently' collect medieval antiquities including ceramics from the University and the City of Oxford as well as from Oxfordshire, and to mark the exact provenance on ordnance survey maps; and this was his 'most original contribution'. He was meticulous at plotting the provenance of his finds, and the plan which he used of the City and University of Oxford 1897 is here used to show the sites mentioned in the text (see Fig. 1). Manning used Plot's county survey as a starting point for his own parish surveys.

After 1900 Manning continued to take an active part on local committees and to record archaeological sites in the City, and he published 'Notes on the archaeology of Oxford and its neighbourhood', the result of work undertaken, with a view to compiling an archaeological survey of Oxfordshire which culminated in a formidable gazetteer now held by the Ashmolean.

In the 1870s scientists studied folklore as well as the natural sciences. In 1895 the ethnographical survey of the British Isles prepared for the British Association for the Advancement of Sciences included archaeology and folklore amongst other disciplines. The Committee of Anthropology appointed Manning to 'direct students with regard to the prosecution of folklore researches in the Oxford district', and he held this position for some years.

Manning's curiosity in folklore may have arisen out of his earlier interest in Oxfordshire industries and customs. In 1897 he published an article entitled 'Oxfordshire Seasonal Festivals' and was 'instrumental in the revival of Morris dancing' in some parts of Oxfordshire. He appears to have been influenced by the seventeenth-century personalities, including the eminent Plot and the 'laborious antiquary' Wood and their writings. Papers given included one on early sports and pastimes in Stuart Oxford illustrated by old prints etc, another on 'William Stokes, Vaulting Master', dealt with a character of the early seventeenth century in Oxford. Stokes had many distinguished pupils in the arts of vaulting and performing sundry gyrations on a dummy horse and published a book on the same. 'Bringing in the Fly', which outlined an ancient tradition, a custom which survived in Wood's time among the cooks of Oxford of making a procession into the woods nearby and

Fig. 68. 'Tavern Relics' on display at the Millenary Exhibition 1912: eighteenth-century English stoneware mugs (left), with medallions of the Angel Inn, and inscription 'Ann King Oxon.' stamped W.R. and crown excise mark, (right) mugs from the Bocardo and Weirs Inn, together with earlier glass bottles. Old Angel Inn 1877.233 and 234; Bocardo 1896.1908 M52; Weirs Inn 1921.224. Courtesy of Bodliean Library.

bringing back a butterfly, was another topic; the history of tennis in the City of Oxford and 'Oxfordshire Village and Peasant Life' were also presented.

The Minute Books of the OAHS record his active involvement on the Topographical Survey sub-committee as from 1905, and the following year he was recording the demolition of Leopold Arms in the City (sometimes referred to as the Bocardo; see Portrait of Lawrence and the Inferences for Oxford's heritage later). At an OAHS meeting he exhibited pottery and glass from the excavations for the foundations of the new premises.

In the same year (1906) Manning also had the foresight to collect oral evidence in the north west of the county from old potting families at the Crown Pottery, Leafield (Fig. 53). George and Alec Franklin (see Part I) were cousins and had learnt the potting trade from their fathers who had in turn followed their father (Henry Franklin d. 1844). Manning sometimes used others to help collect information and artefacts and paid them for their efforts. His account gives

an invaluable insight into the final years of this production centre and of another at Brill in central Buckinghamshire, each with its roots in the medieval period (see Stylistic Development Nineteenth century Oxford earlier).

In 1908 he loaned objects to the Ashmolean. His collection comprised a large number of miscellaneous items in metal, e.g. buckles, cutlery, constables staves as well as one or two pieces of architectural detail and pottery, from no less than forty-seven towns and villages. He also sought parallels for his artefacts in Europe.

Manning was elected Vice President in 1911 and later President of the University Society until June 1914, when its existence was suspended for the duration of the Great War. Cycling opened up new venues, and excursions to archaeological sites were popular with undergraduates in the few years before the war, to which Manning was a party. He chaired the Exhibition Committee on 'The Millenary of the City of Oxford' with great enthusiasm in 1912 and was a 'constant inspiration'. The exhibition illustrated the history and growth of the City from its first mention in the year 912 A.D. in the *Anglo-Saxon Chronicle*, and placed Oxford in the history of the nation (Fig. 68). Manning contributed many exhibits of plans and maps of the City: 'pottery, glass are to be seen in great variety', also the fine puzzle jug in his own possession. He also wrote sections of the catalogue.

This exhibition brought together those with an interest in Oxford's past, both from the City and the University, and included many of the personalities who had contributed to the University collection of medieval and later ceramics curated by the Antiquities Department. In 1914, Manning presented specimens of medieval pottery and other objects from Oxford excavations to the Ashmolean.

He volunteered for the Reserve Battalion of the Oxford and Buckinghamshire Light Infantry in November 1914. His choice of regiment was entirely consistent for a man who had devoted his youthful energies to collecting from these two counties as well as Berkshire. He was too old for active service abroad and instead worked in the docks in Southampton, where in 1917 he contracted pneumonia and died, aged 47. Fortunately, he had bequeathed some and loaned others of his very considerable collection to the Ashmolean, which was secured permanently for the Museum in 1921. At the time his ceramic collection was ranked 'as one of the most important in the country for the study of English medieval ceramics'. Manning's bequest of books left to the Bodleian show no hint that he was interested in technology or how the antiquities that he collected were made, but reflects rather his topographical, folkloric and local history pursuits.

Over the years Manning had collaborated with Herbert Hurst and Arthur Evans, C. F. Bell and E. T. Leeds of the Ashmolean. He was the tangible expression of the strong amateur involvement, and clearly the linch-pin between the undergraduates and the professional archaeological and academic fraternity, providing the continuity of enthusiasm for the subject for some twenty five years.

E. T. Leeds, assistant keeper at the Ashmolean, was also actively involved with the OUAS alongside Manning in the years just before the war. Leeds survived and provided continuity, for future students of archaeology (see Portrait of Lawrence later). Leeds also edited and published posthumously Manning's survey, 'An Archaeological Survey of Oxfordshire', which highlighted 'every available piece of information

about archaeological discoveries in the county'. The Revd. H. E. Salter wrote of him that 'he was a kindly, natural and unassuming friend'. This modest man with prodigious energy had such varied interests including dogs, in particular St. Bernards, but his gifted fieldwork, his 'unrivalled knowledge of Oxfordshire antiquities of every kind' and his enthusiastic collection of artefacts, recorded so consistently during the last decade of the nineteenth and first decade of the twentieth century, provided the Ashmolean with its first truly archaeological medieval and later collection.

Edwardian Collectors

The first decade of the twentieth century was to produce further memorable collections of pottery, whose provenance and collection history have been lost from view. The Ashmolean owes an immense debt to a schoolboy and later undergraduate whose contribution to local archaeology has never been fully appreciated.

— PORTRAIT —

The Informed Amateur Archaeologist – Schoolboy and Undergraduate: T.E. Lawrence.

Like Evans, Thomas Edward (Ned to his family) Lawrence (1888-1935) had shown a deep rooted enthusiasm for medieval and later artefacts when at the age of nine, he undertook his first brass-rubbing of the tomb of a medieval blanket-maker at Witney church, some nine miles from Oxford. Also like Evans, he was much influenced in his early antiquarian interests by his father.

In the fifth form at the Oxford High School for Boys Lawrence and his school friend C. F. Beeson were notorious for their archaeological rummagings'. The fruits of some of these rummagings were first gifted to the Ashmolean in 1906, when the museum was under the direction of Arthur Evans. From the Ashmolean report for 1906 we read ' Owing to the generosity of Mr. E. Lawrence and Mr. C. F. Beeson who have by incessant watchfulness secured everything of antiquarian value which has been found, the most interesting finds have been added to the local antiquities in the museum'. Up to 1905 the Ashmolean had been prepared to purchase artefacts from the city, but thereafter went through a financial crisis. Lawrence's continuing role in enhancing the collection was therefore very timely. While still at school he organised a collection of brass-rubbings belonging to the OAHS and at the age of fifteen was very knowledgable about monumental brasses. His mother's reminscences

Fig. 69. Portrait of Lawrence, detail from photograph, taken by himself, whilst in the sixth form of the Oxford Boys School (1907). He had learnt the skill from his father. Courtesy of Oxfordshire Photographic Archive.

extended across western Europe, but his great passion was English water-colours. He was a proficient photographer and a perfectionist; he is remembered as 'meticulous in recording of information, a trait for which Manning is remembered too. Bell was known to be generous with his knowledge to young people (Kenneth Clark, the late art historian was another of his protégés). Bell's brother also worked in the Art World in America and was very knowledgeable about Oriental Ceramics.

In 1896, the year that the Lawrence family moved to Oxford, Bell joined the Ashmolean as assistant keeper to Arthur Evans, replacing Edward Evans, and his first task was to organise 'the celebrated collection of Renaissance objects of art' belonging to Drury Fortnum.

Up to this time classical antiquity had dominated Oxford scholars' interests, and this new collection was therefore to put Bell at the forefront of academic

recall how he brought back pottery from local building sites to the family home in Polstead Road, north Oxford, and tried to reconstruct the vessels using plasticine!

By 1905 Lawrence was already familiar with the Ashmolean's extensive medieval collection, and would seek 'expert opinion' from one of the Assistant Keepers, Charles Bell, who was particularly interested in medieval pottery. Charles Francis Bell (1871-1966), some seventeen years Lawrence's senior, had family connections on his mother's side with the Pre-Raphaelites, and knew Kelmscott Manor near Lechlade on the Gloucestershire/Oxfordshire border and William Morris's family. He considered himself the last survivor of the pre-Raphaelites. This may have fuelled the young Lawrence's interests in William Morris and 'his beliefs in the pre-industrial values of craftsmanship that led to an admiration for the Middle Ages'. Morris had also been much influenced by the atmosphere of symbolism and medievalism apparent in Oxford in the 1850s and was inspired by the magnificent collection of medieval manuscripts in the Bodleian Library.

Like many of his generation, Bell was very cosmopolitan in outlook and his wide ranging scholarship

Fig. 70. Portrait of C. F. Bell by W. Strang 1913 made shortly after he was appointed the first keeper of the Fine Art Department.

a b c

Fig. 71. Group collected by Lawrence and Beeson from the Civet Cat Cornmarket: wheel-thrown Rhenish drinking vessels with a variety of devices: Details: 71a) the name and arms of 'Jacob Margraf' dated [15]86; 71b) portrait medallion of 'G[r]af Federich' 71c) the arms of Cologne dated 1594; a tripod pipkin and apprentice/money boxes glazed bright green, from the Surrey/Hampshire Border industry. Seventeenth century.

research in an area which would be relevant to Lawrence's collecting. The collection comprised sculptures, painting and glassware, but concentrated mainly on maiolica, bronzes and finger rings. Fortnum had been the acknowledged expert on maiolica (Italian tin-glaze ceramics) in the mid nineteenth century, as well as Bell's friend and his part-sponsor. In 1899 and 1902 Bell rearranged 'The Oxford Room' consisting of 'mediaeval pottery, glass and tiles' as well as the coins and tokens. He also re-labelled the entire series of seventeenth century Oxford City Tradesmens Tokens. Bell's scholarship was to have a profound effect on Lawrence's collecting; Bell understood the importance of maiolica to the visual arts and the delight of handling pots to discover how they were made, and the pleasure in studying motifs and heraldic designs. Some of his tastes will have transmitted themselves to Lawrence.

At the time that Bell first encountered Lawrence he was involved in writing pioneering works on the historical portraits in the University with Mrs Lane Poole (she was married to R. L. Poole, later to become Lawrence's history tutor at Jesus College, Oxford; Poole was the younger son of an Arabic scholar and had gained his Ph. D. at Leipzig), and in 1909 Bell was appointed the first keeper of the newly created Fine Art Department. Thereafter he had little to do with the archaeological side of the museum, but he did supervise Lawrence's undergraduate thesis.

Lawrence's mother recalls 'that his interest was aroused in medieval pottery when some turned up in excavations for a public-house in Cornmarket'. She may have been referring to the site of The Leopold Arms (the Bocardo Prison, no 36 Cornmarket Street) where in 1906 Percy Manning was recording the demolition and the foundations of the cellars (see Portrait of Manning earlier).

Although some dozen near complete vessels were recovered from the Leopold Arms site, there is no evidence from the museum's accessions book at that time to link any of them with Lawrence. In the 1970s Beeson donated some artefacts to the Museum which included a small Rhenish stoneware vessel with portrait medallions which was believed to be from the site of the Leopold Arms. In the same year (1906) Lawrence was collecting whole or near complete vessels from other building sites: at Balliol College he recovered a very fine large medieval cook pot or storage jar (Fig. 3), and from the site of the new Masonic Hall in the High Street a large collection of ceramics

and dated glass bottles of the early eighteenth century (Fig. 51) with some earlier sixteenth-century material. More pots were collected from the site in 1907.

The size of the vessels suggest that Lawrence may have been commissioning workmen to keep the best examples, and his family remembered that he did pay for artefacts out of his pocket. Complete sixteenth-century Rhenish stoneware *Bartmann* jugs were similar to the fragments from the Leopold Arms site and were not parallelled amongst the existing Ashmolean collection.

That same year Lawrence and Beeson rescued much pottery from No. 7 Cornmarket Street — the Civet Cat, a shop on the medieval market frontage and the area behind, belonging to the Cross and Roebuck Inns — where quantities of Rhenish salt-glazed stoneware emerged, the largest group ever recovered from an Oxford site. The *Bartmann* jugs with armorial devices, both real and fake, included two dated examples: 1586 and 1594; they must have interested Bell, and perhaps also a school boy versed in monumental brasses and heraldry. Heraldic symbols provided art historians with an easy method of dating. This Rhenish stoneware collection was later in date than the decorated sixteenth century stonewares from the sites of the Leopold Arms and the new Masonic Hall, and it included more plain straight-necked Frechen jugs, a type often embellished with pewter or even silver mounts. Three apprentice or money boxes with bright green glaze on the upper dome were made at the Surrey/Hampshire production centres as was the tripod pipkin donated by Mrs Lawrence at a much later date (Fig. 71).

Elegant medieval baluster jugs were also retrieved from the site by Lawrence and Beeson. Bell's influence and knowledge of Italian maiolica would have guided Lawrence with the highly decorated Anglo-Netherlandish tin-glaze earthenwares that he retrieved from the Forestry Laboratory site (see later).

Described by his mother as having great energy, Lawrence spent his vacations as a schoolboy and undergraduate cycling great distances, first with his father, later alone, visiting churches and castles in England, Wales and France. Lawrence Senior's interest in church architecture may have stimulated his son's appetite for medieval brasses and castle architecture. The boy's background of regular Sunday school was invaluable to his understanding of the imagery of the medieval world. His visits to churches and castles will have alerted him to aspects of ecclesiastical and secular iconography.

On a visit to Tintern Abbey, in Wales (1907) Lawrence noted encaustic tiles — Manning had collected similar tiles while still an undergraduate in 1890's and R. L. Poole also gifted medieval tiles to the department, but Lawrence noted that 'no pottery seems to have been discovered in the excavations'. More recent archaeological experience confirms the paucity of artefacts associated with monastic areas, but domestic areas of monasteries can be very rich in pottery and other finds.

There is no evidence that Lawrence was a member of the OUAS during his undergraduate years reading Modern History at Jesus College, and like Manning he took as little part in college activities as he could manage. He did his reading in the Bodleian Library, and the breadth and depth of his antiquarian interests impressed those who knew him.

Lawrence's absorbing interest took him constantly to the Ashmolean, and it was here that he met the newly appointed Assistant Keeper E. T. Leeds in 1908 (Fig. 72). Leeds recorded the first meeting with Lawrence 'I set to work on my labels, and a few days later a very youthful figure slid into my sight, enquiring what I was doing'. The enquiry was backed by an impudent yet attractive smile, and the stranger's remarks told me at once that I had to deal with someone, young though he was, who knew the collection far better than I did'. Lawrence's passion of pottery was already well established, but Leeds was able to hone his archaeological skills.

Leeds will have guided him towards the archaeological principles of stratigraphy and chronology, marrying it with historical evidence to give a broader picture. It is noticeable from 1908 that Lawrence begins to gift more medieval pottery to the Museum than previously, perhaps acknowledging Leeds interest in this period rather than the Renaissance-inspired products (the baluster jugs from the Civet Cat were not gifted to the Ashmolean until 1908, while most of the stonewares from the same site had been were presented in 1906; the glass bottles from St Johns College Forestry Laboratory were also presented in 1908 while the Renaissance-inspired tin-glaze earthenware was deposited a year earlier, perhaps reflecting Leeds' greater interest in glass). Lawrence also began to record the depth at which an artefact was found, and to collect fragments of pottery rather than only complete or near complete vessels.

Leeds enlisted Lawrence's help in his 'labels', which was to lead to a lifelong friendship of two people united by a common interest and 'mutual enjoyment' of Ox-

Fig. 72. Portrait of E. T. Leeds *c*.1922 — a stimulating mentor to Lawrence.

ford's past. It was Leeds who first brought Lawrence to the attention of David Hogarth, a professional archaeologist who replaced Arthur Evans as Keeper at the Ashmolean at the end of 1908, freeing Evans to dedicate himself to his Mediterranean excavations. In 1909 Lawrence volunteered his services to 'organise and re-label the somewhat heterogeneous collections of medieval antiquities', which included some of Manning's loaned objects. Leeds was responsible for updating much of the accessioning which had not been carried out systematically since 1896. Most of Lawrence's gifts were catalogued at this time (1909). Later his mother donated more of his ceramic collection, particularly from the sites of the Civet Cat and the new Masonic Hall.

Within a month of starting work at the Ashmolean, Lawrence wanted to carry out a 'watching brief' on the excavations for the quatercentenary buildings of Brasenose College on its High Street frontage, but was discouraged from it because 'research into mediaeval

Fig. 73. Redwares: new shapes for the table – multi-handled drinking vessel; a well glazed bowl possibly copying metal, wood or a glass vessel; and a skillet in the medieval tradition all from shops or domestic dwellings predating the Brasenose Quatercenterary building. A fragment of a contemporary 'mantle', an open topped vessel, suggests that distillation processes were carried out nearby (not illustrated). Seventeenth century. Brasenose 1909.1095, 1096 and 1896-1908. (Ht. 10.5 cm.; 6.5 cm.; 4.0 cm.).

pottery was not a recognised part of the University's curriculum'. Some desirable pieces were however deposited with the Museum (see Stylistic development Seventeenth Century Stuart Oxford earlier for redwares and Fig. 73).

In the long vacation of 1909, in preparation for his undergraduate thesis Lawrence walked 1,100 miles through Syria studying crusader castles, in the hottest two months of the year. His letters home show him still to be close to his family, but they also display a wry sense of humour: 'Why can't somebody invent an occupation for flies? They have too much leisure'. After this amazing feat of endurance Lawrence was back in Oxford and Leeds persuaded him to tell Hogarth of his travels. Hogarth was impressed.

The excavations at the Radcliffe Camera book stack were under way at this time and 'Naturally they drew Lawrence like a magnet'. Both Leeds and Lawrence were keen to obtain any stratigraphic evidence that might be useful, and some old labels still testify to their diligence 'T. E. L. brought handle of green glaze, 14ft down at Camera' (1909.1173a). The Camera excavations produced a wealth of artefactual material.

Lawrence's grasp of Oxford collections is illustrated by a letter from abroad. A private collection formed by F. C. Wellstood, an assistant in the Bodleian Library, had special merits and included many bottles. Lawrence wrote to Leeds, on learning that Wellstood was moving away from Oxford, asking: 'Is it worthwhile getting

casts of their stamps do you think? Mr Jackson has none exchangeable'. Jackson also had a considerable collection from the site (see Portrait of Jackson later). It was the practise to have casts made where possible of specimens in other hands.

The results of new ceramic acquisitions formed the basis of a paper on medieval pottery which Leeds gave to the OAHS at the beginning of 1910. Entitled 'Medieval Pottery found in Oxford', it reflects the interest in these excavations by both gown and town.

Later that year Lawrence obtained a First Class degree and was intent on sitting for a B. Litt., entitled *Mediaeval lead-glazed Pottery, from the 11th to the 16th Centuries*. He set out on his bicycle to seek the principal collections outside London, at Bristol, Hanley in Staffordshire (which had a long tradition of pottery making, first recorded by Plot in 1686), and York amongst others. Lawrence's itinerary may have been planned with the aid of Jewitt's *The Ceramic Art of Great Britain* published in 1878 — two very comprehensive volumes used by Fortnum, Bell and Leeds in their researches.

In the summer Lawrence also visited Bayeux in France with his two brothers. In the museum there his brother recalled that whilst he had 'tried to draw a piece of the tapestry bearing upon his pottery, I (Will) acted as a decoy in another direction. They got enough notes for him to reconstruct it all right in private'. He also visited Reims. In the autumn, he returned to France to view the pottery collection at Rouen, from where Leeds received a letter informing him that he (Leeds) had been appointed to supervise Lawrence's research. A fortnight later however, Lawrence departed to join the British Museum archaeological expedition to the ancient Hittite city of Carchemish (now in Turkey), a post which Hogarth was instrumental in engineering for him.

A year later in the autumn of 1911, Lawrence helped Leeds make a selection of pottery from the city for display in the 'Oxford Millenary Exhibition', which necessitated a visit to a retired academic, Thomas W. Jackson, to view his collection from the Radcliffe Camera. Leeds apparently felt he needed Lawrence's support, for Jackson, one of Benjamin Jowett's protégés, had been one of the greatest opponents of the amalgamation between the University Galleries and the Ashmolean in 1908. The younger men were amazed by the volume of sherds that Jackson had amassed from the Radcliffe Camera, and they managed to come away with a few examples for the great exhibition. (See Portrait of Jackson later).

Mrs Lawrence also contributed pots collected by her son to the very extensive exhibition and that same year Leeds nominated her to the OAHS.

By 1912 Lawrence was back in Carchemish, and Leeds realised that Lawrence's thesis on medieval pottery was doomed.

Lawrence was visually astute, a careful observer of all he saw, always accompanied by a sketch book on his travels, in which he planned and drew, though he did not perceive himself as a real artist. He collected picture post-cards and later he added a camera to his sparse archaeological tool-kit. He had considerable charm and a facility for friendships which encouraged many gifted people into his orbit.

Lawrence, Leeds and on occasions Bell continued to correspond about tile, pottery and sack-bottles, a correspondance which was to continue throughout the Great War. After the war, Lawrence returned to Oxford in 1919 and a three year scholarship at All Soul's College to write the story of his Arabian campaign. He continued his close relationship with the Antiquities Department, enthusing Leeds in 1920 to take an interest in the exceptional collection of wine bottles in the cellars of All Souls (some seven hundred bottles all with stamps of the College Common Room dating to the eighteenth and nineteenth centuries).

Leeds was already an authority on Oxford taverns, their license-holders and wine bottles. He had worked out a system for dating the first English glass wine bottles, covering the period 1650–1720. Through documentary research in the City and University archives, he identified many bottle stamps from Oxford excavations with the licensees of city taverns. 'When arranged by date according to licence, the bottles fell into a perfect typological sequence capable of application to unstamped bottles found in all parts of the country'.

After All Souls, Lawrence served first in the Tank Corps and then in the ranks of the Air Force, in both cases under assumed names. His links with the Ashmolean had lessened but he wrote to Bell in 1930: 'It's the only place in Oxford which makes me feel homesick' and Leeds recalls that his visits there 'brought an encouraging enthusiasm into a placid and rather un-eventful backwater'.

Shortly after his discharge from the Air Force in 1935, Lawrence died in a motor-cycle accident. E. M. Forster wrote a portrait of him: 'If when the schoolboy grows up he takes to archaeology seriously, he seldom loses this primitive excitement, this thrill of adventure, reinforcing the thrill of research'. Leeds liked to think that he might have returned to 'this former field of activity, which he had never forgotten'.

Lawrence's passion for brass-rubbing, church architecture, castles, medieval and later pottery and seventeenth-eighteenth century wine bottles, places him amongst the great amateur archaeologists of the Edwardian era - a very different facet of 'Lawrence of Arabia'.

Another personality, working in a room underneath the Bodleian Library at the time when excavations for the underground bookstore at the north side of the Radcliffe Camera were underway, was like Leeds and Lawrence aware of the immense archaeological potential of the site. His proximity to the site resulted in the biggest single collection of a superb group of ceramics, all predating the building of the Radcliffe Camera in 1737.

— PORTRAIT —

Academic and Collector of Prints and Ceramics: T. W. Jackson.

Thomas Watson Jackson, (c.1838-1914), read *Literae Humaniores* at Balliol College (1858-1862), where he was an Exhibitioner, senior fellow of Worcester College (1864). Later he held college posts of Dean and Vice Provost (1877); he was remembered by a former pupil as an 'admirable teacher ... he possessed in full measure that rare gift of helping his pupils by showing them how to use their own judgement'. He was chosen to sit on a new body of curators of the University Galleries in 1884, and served on a sub-committee which took charge of the collection of plaster casts, used to teach undergraduates classical form and style which epitomised the nineteenth-century emphasis on a classical education. This collection is 'one of the oldest and best preserved in Britain'.

The provisional Catalogue of the Paintings (1891), which placed on record a 'well informed synthesis', was largely written by Jackson, 'one of the best known figures in artistic circles in Oxford' (Fig. 74). But perhaps his most important work, undertaken on behalf of the Bodleian, was the re-cataloguing of a great part of the enormously rich Douce collection, which he rescued from 'neglect and disorder' (Figs. 37 and 56). Francis Douce (1757–1834), an eccentric antiquary, had collected material illustrating the manners and customs of all ages. Jackson, like Manning, was himself an enthusiastic amateur and eclectic collector of prints. He also dedicated the 'same toil and patience'

Fig. 74. Pencil drawing of Thomas Watson Jackson –
a sympathetic tutor but a fierce opponent of the amalgamation of the University Galleries and the Ashmolean.
Private Collection, Courtauld Institute of Art.

to making an elaborate slip catalogue of the Hope Collection, of which he became Keeper in 1897 (see Fig. 75). He was a curator of the Bodleian Library, as well as of the University Galleries before its amalgamation with the Ashmolean.

Jackson was for many years a very active member of the standing committee of the Visitors, which directed the affairs of the University Galleries before the enactment of the new Ashmolean statute (1908). As we have seen he took a jaundiced view of the amalgamation of the Museum and Galleries: he identified himself closely with what he imagined to be the interests of the latter, while Evans spearheaded the amalgamation.

Jackson had known Evans since the latter was a young man in the 1870s, and was elected to the OAHS a year before Evans in 1873. He had a warm appreciation of Bell and wrote of him that he was 'a most accomplished and devoted student of art'. He may have known of Manning by reputation if not at first hand through his connections with the Ashmolean Museum, and possibly through their mutual interest in the

collection of prints, and he was known to Leeds and Lawrence; Leeds regarded the older man with some trepidation (see Portrait of Lawrence earlier).

Over the years Jackson had collected sherds and tiles from building sites and donated them to the Ashmolean, including material from under the site of Carfax Church where they are recorded as being Celtic, Roman and Medieval. The latter included an 'enamelled copper plaque with beautiful foliated design of thirteenth-century' probably made in Limoges, and four Saxon silver pennies dated to the first half of the tenth century. The scholarly Jackson gifted many books to the Ashmolean in the 1900s. They reflect the breadth of his European knowledge of pictures, but also included Japanese art and biographies of English artists and craftsmen: Turner, Ruskin and William Morris. Jackson collected or purchased ceramics from behind the 'unsightly hoarding in the Radcliffe Square' (Fig. 81), which resulted in the largest private medieval and later ceramic collection to be bequeathed to the Ashmolean: a magnificent group of seventeenth and eighteenth-century ceramics, which would have delighted Douce and which extended the range of the department's collection.

Fig. 75. An engraving (detail) 'The Market Place at Watlington, Oxon.,' after F. McKenzie by W. and J. Skelton 1825, showing a range of pottery vessels for sale. Jackson curated the Hope Collection from 1897.

Leeds reported how he and Lawrence had been 'overwhelmed by the masses of sherds that Jackson had collected, all sorted out according to fabric and ornamentation in the lids of dress-boxes'. When after a long illness, Jackson died in 1914, Leeds approached the executors and the pottery collection was passed to the Ashmolean. Bell sadly disposed of many of Jackson's Bodleian 'memoranda and notebooks and the receipted bills of the Hope Collection for 1911'. As a man Jackson was remembered with affection by his pupils many of whom 'owe more than we can ever hope to acknowledge', but through his public service to the university he was perceived more as a 'dauntless and resolute fighter', an active disputant in Oxford's scholastic tradition.

Other contemporary collectors included A. B. Emden, later to become the distinguished medievalist and historian of universities, who also contributed ceramics from the Radcliffe Camera excavations, in particular teawares in Chinese porcelain and tin-glaze earthenware imitations decorated in the Chinese style in underglaze blue. On occasions, he recorded their exact provenance, which was carefully transcribed to the appropriate accessions book in the Ashmolean. He was later immortalized in a be-spectacled gargoyle at St Edmund Hall.

Post World War I Collectors

After the Great War very little pottery was added during the 1920s. Manning was gone and with him a whole generation of potential enthusiasts. Leeds tried to take up where Manning had left off, and as we have seen came to form a bridge between the undergraduates and the professional archaeologists. Leeds in particular was much liked by 'successive generations of Oxford students', and one site in the City was to draw in the next generation, many of whom later became professional archaeologists. Their vision was to dominate archaeological thinking until the last decades of the twentieth century.

— PORTRAIT —

Professional Archaeological Field-worker and Art Historian: R. L. S. Bruce-Mitford

Rupert Leo Scott Bruce-Mitford (1914–1994) was born of Anglo-Canadian parents at the beginning of the Great War. As an archaeologist he was essentially an 'objects man', but became a notable field-worker too. His father died when he was only four years of

age. In his later school life at Christ's Hospital in London he shared some similarities with Lawrence, in that both were coached in classics and mathematics respectively by elder brothers, and both switched to history as an alternative option (Bruce-Mitford was to become a great admirer of Lawrence). At the age of sixteen or seventeen he too recognised that he was attracted by 'concrete and visual' things, when he discovered medieval art. 'The pre-requisite for an archaeologist, I was to discover, is a love of objects'.

Bruce-Mitford came up to Hertford College with a history scholarship in 1933, and was attracted to the oldest part of the Bodleian Library. Here he became fascinated with a twelfth-century bestiary and 'after some weeks I could stand my ignorance and quell my curiosity no longer' and approached the interior of Duke Humphrey's Library to ask for it. In his vacations he would often use the Reading Room of the British Museum, and when in need of a change would tack onto the Guide Lecturers showing visitors round the building, absorbing information on specific items from differing cultures.

Fig. 76. Portrait of Rupert Bruce-Mitford taken at the beginning of the Second World War *c.* 1939, shortly after he had published the New Bodleian site. Courtesy of Margaret Bruce-Mitford.

Fig. 77. Wheel-thrown 'painted' pitchers from a well group rescued by Bruce-Mitford. First half of thirteenth century. New Bodleian 1937.451, 446 and 450. (Ht. 27.5 cm.; incomplete; 29.5 cm.).

After graduating he spent 1937–8 at the Ashmolean re-arranging and displaying the medieval pilgrim badges. It was during this time that the builders began to dig a 'huge hole, lined with interlocked sheet piles', at the junction of Broad Street and Parks Road, for the foundations of the New Bodleian Library. William Pantin had previously recorded the above ground archaeology (the vernacular architecture), and Bruce-Mitford, sometimes aided by John Daniel and Martyn Jope, rescued and salvaged finds.

Bruce-Mitford's painstaking research, the first serious study of medieval pottery, gave a chronological sequence of pottery for Oxford that has never had to be challenged, although refined and extended (Fig. 77). 'The Bodleian site was particularly fortunate both in its material and its excavator, who saw a potential which others might have failed to recognise'.

After his brief spell at the Ashmolean, the diligent Bruce-Mitford joined the staff of the British Museum in 1938, where one of his first assignments was to attend a Sale Room and bid for 'a fine green and red-striped medieval pot'. Later he set up the National Reference Collection of Dated Medieval Sherds in the British Museum, where in 1954 he became Keeper of Medieval and Later Antiquities. He continued there all his working life, curating and researching its medieval collections and inspiring future young scholars. Later he took up formal University teaching.

He wrote in an account of his career: 'archaeology is not just excavation, the making of discoveries by digging... Apart from the diggers there are the analysts and systematizers of the materials, the interpreters as well as the finders. Some people are both'. Bruce-Mitford's

description could almost be a self-portrait, and his 'passionate commitment' to the subject was with him to the very end.

In 1938, John Daniel, who had collaborated with Bruce-Mitford on the Bodleian site, voluntarily spent a considerable portion of his time watching excavations and collecting pottery and other small finds on behalf of the Ashmolean. Daniel also made records when a tunnel was dug to connect the old Bodleian building with its new extension across Broad Street. This produced numerous small finds, especially in the Clarendon Quadrangle where the trench cut across the City Wall and ditch (see also Part I Seventeenth Century Oxford). Daniel was also on hand when pottery was rescued from the back of the Fleur-de-Luce (117-9 St. Aldates; see Part I Seventeenth Century Oxford).

With the advent of the Second World War, archaeology had largely migrated from the hands of enthusiastic amateurs to those of professionals whose discipline established a framework for others to build on. The most notable locally was Martyn Jope, active in the OUAS (1937-1940) and President of the Society in 1938, whose contribution to the subject during the 1940s and 1950s was far in advance of its time and who built on Bruce-Mitford's work at the New Bodleian (see earlier and Part I Methods of Manufacture).

The archaeological investigations at that time were co-ordinated at the Ashmolean Museum. Jope continued to build up a chronology, bringing together all the techniques of the discipline; drawing on historical,

Fig. 78. 'The Angel' Hotel (site of New Examination Schools) c. 1840. Manning exhibited an engraving of the inn at the OAHS exhibition in 1894 and at the Millenary Exhibition in 1912. Courtesy of Bodleian Library.

archaeological, scientific and technological evidence to give a more balanced picture of medieval life set in a dated framework. The results of his work in the City are largely published in the county journal, *Oxoniensia* and in *Dark Age Britain*, a volume of essays dedicated to E. T. Leeds.

These colourful individuals, with their contrasting personalities and different family circumstances, all found obvious enjoyment in the past. Their original minds and intellectual energy, acute visual sense and power of observation also displayed a sensitivity towards people and their achievements, manners, customs and folklore, which led to an appreciation of objects, and some were intrigued by the technical skills associated and the craftsmen behind the artefact. The potter's craft communicates all these qualities and connects people and ideas, and as such is the key to understanding the periods in which the pots were made. The appreciation of these early collectors was initially stimulated by family or peers; the changing face of Oxford with demolitions and building sites, open on occasions over a number of years, provided the material culture that kindled their interest in those formative years between nine years of age and their late teens; the presence of the Ashmolean, a University Museum of national and international standing, encouraged their growing interest.

These pre-World War I collectors were also capable of being very determined in their endeavours! The increasing mobility in Plot's England with the introduction of new modes of travel coincided with a growth in the antiquarian spirit which were originally influenced by the classical revival in Renaissance Italy. The archaeological excavations of classical sites in the Mediterranean and the colonial expansion in the Victorian period revived this spirit. During the Edwardian era it was the popularity of the bicycle that opened up England and continental Europe to a new generation of enthusiasts. These voyages of adventure and discovery nurtured a fresh enthusiasm as well as a wider perspective which gave a new impetus, leading to the collection of ceramic artefacts and the study of the potter's craft at a time when everything was becoming mass-produced by machine. These Oxford men, in particular Lawrence, were influenced by the Medievalism of the Pre-Raphaelites, who in turn were much inspired by the atmosphere of Oxford in the mid nineteenth century. The enthusiasm of these young collectors was nurtured by the staff at the Ashmolean either through their participation at the University Society's meetings, through their membership of the OAHS or by direct contact in the Museum.

Fig. 79. A wheel-thrown *Bartmann* dated '1660' with a merchant medallion 'P.V.A.' — a device belonging to Pieter van der Ancher, a dutch merchant residing in London *c*.1660. He specialised in French and Rhenish wine and beer from Bremen in north Germany. The jug was recovered from the site of the Old Angel Inn 1914.632. (Ht. 30 cm.).

There has inevitably been some bias in the collecting. Manning and even Lawrence, on occasions, collected individual items of interest (Lawrence was possibly drawn to shelled lamps, Rhenish stonewares, tin-glaze earthenwares and glass bottles in particular), while Emden showed a preference for the white translucent porcelain and tin-glaze earthenware tea-wares. Evans and Jackson appear to have been less eclectic and their collections are a more complete record of the below-ground deposits of their respective sites. Evans, Manning and Bruce-Mitford communicated the results of their discoveries to the general public through lectures, exhibitions, reports to the press and definitive publications so drawing in the next generation. These pioneer collectors and Oxford's first amateur archaeologists and their collections combine to make a very substantial University collection of medieval and later ceramics.

Conclusions for Historic Oxford

The Ashmolean collections were neglected during the eighteenth century. One of the museum's most respected and scholarly keepers wrote: 'You will perhaps laugh to see me tri[f]ling about a Place now despised and undervalued — and when soe little encouragement is given *here* to labours of this kind'. It was not until the 1830s, some 150 years after Plot had taken up his curatorship, that the museum began to regain its reputation, and initially very small collections of locally made earthenware pottery began to be presented to the museum by the University.

These collections reflect a wide range of sites — rubbish pits and primary fills of wells associated with domestic dwellings and shops, academic halls, a principal's residence, a prison, taverns and coaching inns, all mirroring the changing social history and the differing levels of society of both town and university. The earthenware vessels were carefully catalogued and are variously described as 'ancient earthen vessels', 'of very rude workmanship' or even on one occasion as 'barbarous'. Similar adjectives to describe medieval artefacts were used in seminal papers at national level too.

The process of formation of the collection had been lost from view, because the ceramics are now stored by type reflecting their production centres. For the purpose of this study the complete or near complete vessels pre 1940 were recorded on a database and sorted by site groups, and then linked where possible to the topographical and historical evidence. It is possible now to view the collections digitally and sort them into whatever patterning is appropriate to particular new research, without physically moving them in the store. Some provisional results can be considered at this stage as follows:-

Inferences for Oxford's Medieval Heritage

This survey of the collection has identified significant new archaeological information in many places. Pottery recorded in the 1890s as Late Celtic vessels from a number of sites (St. Mary's Entry, Carfax Church (see Portrait of Jackson earlier) and Radcliffe Camera in 1909/1910 is now known to be late Saxon in date (tenth – eleventh centuries). This is the period when Oxford appears first in both the historical and archaeological records. In 1935, 18-20 Cornmarket Street was demolished to reveal the first evidence of late Saxon industrial activity at what might be expected

Fig. 80. The shop 'The Civet Cat' and adjoining buildings in 1907, taken by Henry Taunt. The area behind belonged to two inns, and the discarded Rhenish stonewares were probably associated with robust living in the later sixteenth and seventeenth century. Courtesy of Oxfordshire Photographic Archive.

to have been the commercial hub of the town. These were crucibles, used in metal smelting, and were similar to those from a peripheral area at the Old Angel Inn Hotel (See Stylistic Development section Eleventh Century Oxford earlier).

The significance of these early finds needs to be evaluated with care, because of the limited supporting information. The Old Angel Inn is a case in point, where the new Examination Schools were completed in 1882. From 1391 to 1510 there had been a small inn called the Tabard, which became one of the three great inns of Oxford in the sixteenth century, Oxford's first Coffee House in 1651 (No. 85 High Street), and remained the city's most important coaching inn into the nineteenth century.

The labourers digging the site recovered artefacts, but did not have the benefit of a purchaser connected with the Ashmolean, and the majority found their way across the High Street to an antique dealer whose shop resembled 'a medievalist's Aladdin's cave'. Inevitably these were to be scattered across the country, and many are now traceable to national and regional museums (see Part I Fig. 25 and the highly decorated puzzle jug in the Stylistic Development section Thirteenth–Fourteenth Century Oxford). T. G. Jackson as supervising architect did oversee the emptying of some pits, and Herbert Hurst inspected others. The university authorities sent fragments of Romano-British, Saxon, medieval and later pottery to the Ashmolean, and the few earlier items (eleventh or thirteenth century) from the Examinations Schools site are significant for understanding urban development at this remote end of the High Street, the majority probably associated with the Angel itself (from 1510).

More centrally in the medieval town, pots rescued in the construction of the new Town Hall in St Aldate's (1893-97) include thirteenth century ceramic vessels which could originate from a house belonging to a wealthy Jew in the thirteenth century. The spotlight returned to this area in 1938 when medieval and later pottery was excavated from parts of the Fleur-de-Luce, earlier the site of Battes Inn, which adjoined the Swyndlestock (the precursor to the Mermaid). This had been one of many houses owned by Oxford Jews, Jacob the Jew in 1270, and a highly decorated stout baluster jug from the site dates to this period.

Moving north on medieval Cornmarket Street, a 'fancy repository' at No. 7 Cornmarket, The Civet Cat, stood next to the Old Roebuck Hotel. (The Civet Cat was the trade sign used by perfumers). Lawrence and his school friend C. F. Beeson rescued medieval and later pottery from the area beneath the shop and the area behind, belonging to the Cross Inn or on the other side to the Roebuck Inn (Figs. 71 and 80).

The medieval finds may have come from the bottom of a well, which fell into disuse and was filled up behind the selds, belonging to Harding Hall (c.1376 AD).

The biggest and most tantalising of the pre-1940 groups in Oxford was rescued during the excavation for the underground bookstore of the Bodleian Library in Radcliffe Square. This was an area which had lain

Fig. 81. The Bodleian bookstore excavations, surrounded by a hoarding c. 1910, with the Radcliffe Camera behind. Courtesy of Bodleian Library.

71

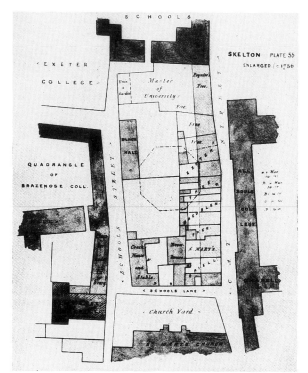

Fig. 82. Schools Street and much of Catte Street as destroyed by the building of the Camera prior to 1737. Reproduced by Herbert Hurst, a local antiquary, from Skelton's original *c.*1756. Jackson's magnificent ceramic collection was derived from the area to the north of the octagonal outline. Courtesy of Bodleian Library.

in May 1910 the last of '8,032 loads' of earth were carted away.

This bookstore site included the foundations of Black Hall, a building nineteen feet in width from west to east with 'a well-preserved tiled passage ...' 'whilst underneath, fourteen foot below street level, was a chamber which was probably a cellar. At the back of the north east corner of the hall was a bed of wood ashes at least eight foot deep, in which were found much broken pottery and many bones'. The foundations of several more buildings fell within the perimeter of the excavations; their substructure extended some eighteen feet below the present street level, built at different angles than the later foundations. At least seven stone constructed wells and stone-lined rubbish pits measuring six foot by four foot were found behind where the houses had formerly been. Their foundations were on the gravel at water level, 'eighteen foot six inches below the surface'. The material recovered in 1909 included pottery from the eleventh century through to *c.*1737,

unused since being bought up piecemeal and cleared for building the Radcliffe Camera in 1737. This major change to the topography at the heart of the University was revealed in 1912 when Manning exhibited Skelton's plan of 1756 showing the cleared houses, courts and rows of tenements (Fig. 82). The area had traditionally been associated with parchment makers, illuminators and bookbinders of the university, also a brewhouse and a tavern; Hogarth's engraving 'An Election Entertainment' *c.*1755 gives us a taste of such an interior of the period with chafing dishes, platters, pitchers, sack-bottles, glasses and clay-pipes.

Unlike previous excavations the bookstore is barely mentioned in the Minute Books of the OAHS, and Manning does not give his customary round-up of excavations and finds for that year. However, a series of photographs by W. P. Ellis show stages of progress, many taken from the Picture Gallery overlooking the excavations. These postcards belonged to F. Madan, the Librarian of the Bodleian, and they provide some information on the progress of the construction work;

Fig. 83. Engraving of two baluster jugs and two bottles, believed to be deliberately buried *c.*1290 in the foundation of the walls of Trinity College, formerly Durham Hall. A medieval time capsule. These vessels were amongst the first medieval pottery to be presented to the Museum in 1838. Trinity College 1836.1868 p17.

Fig. 84. South Parks Road, north east corner of New Bodleian library site where Bruce-Mitford carried out rescue excavations, He isolated well groups, pit groups and related the below-ground archaeology with the topographic and historical record wherever possible. Digging foundations (Wadham College in the background). Courtesy of Bodleian Library.

after which the clearance for the Camera gives a firm *terminus ante quem* for the area (see Stylistic Development section Eighteenth Century Georgian Oxford earlier).

Sites to the north tell us of the suburban expansion of the medieval town. The site of the Randolph Hotel occupied medieval tenements which fronted St Giles, the earliest pottery was thirteenth century in date. One of the four vessels found buried at Trinity College (a baluster jug) contained a coin whose date corresponded with the inclosure of *c.*1290, suggesting that these vessels had been buried deliberately at the time of the foundation of Durham College, for Benedictine monks (see Part I for What more can we learn from these pots?).

Medieval extramural development was also confirmed in a major university development begun in 1936, one of England's first urban 'rescue excavations'. Here houses and shops were cleared at the north east end of Broad Street and at the south west end of South Parks Road for the basement excavations for the New Bodleian Library. Bruce-Mitford wrote: 'They took everything out over a large area down to twenty five feet, onto the clay.

The medieval houses on the Broad Street frontage had each had a well, or a succession of wells, on the narrow strip of land that ran back from the frontage, dug down through the Thames gravel to the level of the clay. The well bottoms all had fillings of two or three feet of mud. These mud cylinders were full of broken medieval pottery, handleless jugs, bowls, and

odds and ends. We could not hold up the mechanical diggers, but I was put in charge of watching the site. My job was then to jump on the lorry and sitting on the pile, as it drove through the city to some gravel hungry site at Cumnor, pick out all the bits of medieval pottery I could find, put them in a bag, and come back on the bus or in an empty lorry. I took my spoil to the Ashmolean where in an upper room I washed the sherds and stuck them together. Later I would have to study them, make drawings and publish an account. This was excellent training and experience on the job, thrown in head first, dealing all the time with new and original materials, at first hand. It was a taste of rescue archaeology before that term was invented. It was also great fun'.

In 1937 an exhibition of objects, photographs, plans and water-colour drawings, illustrative of the past history of the site of the New Bodleian, was on view for three months during the summer. The site had produced a large medieval collection of complete or near complete vessels, pots covering a similar temporal span to those from Radcliffe Square. This time, however, the precise location of individual finds was recorded.

Inferences for Oxford's Post-Medieval Heritage

The site of the Old Angel Inn had provided the first substantial groups for the medieval period, and it was another High Street site which provided the first substantial post-medieval collection. This was Oriel College's commercial development which laid out

Fig. 85. Properties on the south side of the High Street, became the site of King Edward Street *c.*1870. Courtesy of the Bodleian Library.

Fig. 86. Moulded and wheel-thrown slipwares from the Staffordshire and Bristol potteries, and tin-glaze earthenwares made in London, Liverpool and the Netherlands; much of it collected in December 1874, during the laying out of King Edward Street. Evans Collection.

King Edward Street in 1871-5, removing several High Street shops and houses to create a new street with shops.

Swan Court was removed in 1871 and had public houses at either end. This development produced the first sizable collection of seventeenth-century refuse with some fifteenth or early sixteenth and eighteenth-century pieces, including pottery, clay pipes, glass bottles, some wine bottles with vintner's stamps, metalwork and tradesmens tokens, all reflecting considerable wealth and social status of the former owners. The range of tin-glaze earthenwares in particular is unparalleled elsewhere in the city (Fig. 86).

The King Edward Street collection was to form the nucleus of the medieval and later collection. Many of these vessels can probably be associated with shops and inns on the site, the Swan on the Hoop and St. Thomas's Head, and possibly the rear of Tackley's Inn (No. 107 High Street). The latter had been an academic hall, its cellar used as a tavern during the fourteenth and fifteenth centuries. To the west (of the

Tavern) lay a grammar hall known as Buckley Hall, with shops in front which were leased in 1549 to a protestant refugee from Holland. His business was bookselling, and the cellar was used as a wine shop which continued until the end of seventeenth century when it became a coffee house.

Tackley's Inn subsequently became the residence of James Pen, a chandler and manciple of St. John's College. Pen died in 1642, and his probate inventory show that a variety of glass vessels and tin-glaze earthenwares were becoming available in Oxford in the mid seventeenth century. The 'curiosities' which would later reach the Ashmolean were purchased by an inquisitive undergraduate from workmen demolishing the buildings and preparing the ground-surface; Arthur Evans was to become Keeper of the museum (see earlier).

Colleges such as Christ Church, Hertford, Lincoln and University College continued to expand during the second half of the nineteenth century to accommodate increasing numbers of undergraduates and gave small but useful collections to the Ashmolean.

Three sites have unusual collections of post-medieval pottery, Civet Cat and Bocardo in Cornmarket Street and the new Masonic Hall site in the High Street, each have vessels and fragments of late sixteenth century German stonewares, some with portrait medallions.

They are much better represented here than on any other excavated site in the city, but it is still unclear what is the common denominator between for instance the new Masonic Hall site and the town gaol. The Bocardo finds came from the 1906 demolition of the Leopold Arms (36 Cornmarket Street), where

Fig. 87. The Masonic Hall site on the north side of the High Street with the chapel of St Edmund Hall. This area was open ground from about 1900, the new building being completed in 1908. Courtesy of Bodleian Library.

Fig. 88. An engraving of The North Gate, known as The Bocardo after a drawing by J. B. Malchair *c.* 1770. The Leopold Arms site included the west (left) side of the gatehouse. Manning Collection. Courtesy of Bodleian Library.

foundations in its cellar were identified by Manning as the south west corner of what had been the town prison, where the martyred Bishops Cranmer, Latimer and Ridley had been held.

The prison was shown to have been constructed on the fill of the pre-existing town ditch on the west side of the North Gate. It is not clear if the finds came from inside or outside the prison, but some were clearly associated with it (see Chas. Cook's mug Fig. 89), and the artefacts possibly related to both gaolers and felons.

Close to the Civet Cat was the 'Painted Room' at No 3 Cornmarket Street, reprieved from demolition and the source of a late sixteenth-century or early seventeenth-century drinking vessel and apprentice box (Fig. 38 in the foreground). This site had been an inn since 1370 and in 1604 documents show it was occupied by John Davenant, a friend of William Shakespeare who later became godfather to Davenant's son.

Fig. 89. Wheel-thrown red earthenwares, glazed internally; London stonewares including a pint mug inscribed 'Chas. Cook - Bocardo'; local slipware platters and salt-glazed stoneware teacups from the north Midlands. All pre-date the demolition of the Bocardo in 1771 AD; some illustrated from the site were gifted to the Museum by Manning.

Fig. 90. Looking south down St. Aldates, with the sign of the Fleur-de-Luce in the background. The area behind the tavern was to produce an exotic seventeenth century collection. In the foreground to the right can be seen the Butter Market. Manning Collection. Courtesy of Bodleian Library.

Many Oxford sites have special associations with what was perhaps the city's most famous decade, the 1640s when it housed the royalist garrison in the Civil War. The Fleur-de-Luce at Carfax (the fleur-de-lis insignia had been a medieval symbol of loyalty to the Royal House) was leased to Anthony Wood's family at this time, and the catastrophic fire of 1645 which swept much of the west of the walled town consumed the stables and back-houses of this property. The majority of the pottery from the site dates to the early-mid seventeenth century and includes some interesting continental imports (see Part I Seventeenth Century Stuart Oxford). (The property is frequently referred to in the *Life and Times* of Anthony Wood).

Another source of finds of the Civil War period is the city ditch, which was used as a vast tip soon after the siege of Oxford. The tunnel dug to connect the Bodleian Library with its new extension across Broad Street produced numerous finds from the slighted ditch. A less easily explained source of a very similar period is a large pit on part of St Johns College in Parks Road (the Forestry Laboratory) collected by Lawrence. The ceramic containers from this site may be associated with college living (Fig. 91), and it is interesting to note that at this time St John's manciple or housekeeper, James Pen, was also a successful chandler/grocer in the High Street, who was buying in tin-glaze earthenware as shown by his probate inventory (above, Tackleys Inn).

Excavations in 1899 of the Clarendon Building Enclosure set out to investigate the medieval defences but the surviving artefacts relate to the last flowering of this defensive system and fragments of Rhenish stonewares suggest a mid-late seventeenth century date.

The collections also include later material. A dump ten foot down at Carfax was possibly on part of the Mermaid Inn, and yielded a group which extended the range of the existing Ashmolean collection into the early nineteenth century. It included for the first time the mass-produced wares brought to Oxford from the North Staffordshire factories (Fig. 92).

Much in the reserve collection remains unpublished, and the collections dating to the sixteenth, seventeenth and eighteenth century are particularly illuminating for consumer preferences and the cultural history of the City in cases where they can be reconstructed into original assemblages. The chronologically significant contexts need to be analysed further along with other material culture from these same assemblages in order to provide a more in-depth historical picture. More recent archaeological excavations have had to build up chronologies based on the geological finger-printing of small sherds, adapted to study the raw materials used in pottery production, as only one or two complete profiles of pottery vessels might be expected in as many as 10,000 sherds.

These collections have never been surpassed and will remain invaluable to future students.

This guide has attempted to highlight the major unpublished medieval and later collections housed in the Department of Antiquities (a data-base can be consulted for the numerous smaller collections, not mentioned), largely collected during the last decades of the nineteenth and first decade of the twentieth century. This was a particularly dynamic period for Oxford's archaeology when academic and field-worker collaborated. Despite the possible biases in the collection there are substantial differences (specifically Rhenish stonewares and tin-glaze earthenwares) in the pottery used by the townsmen based in the commercial centre, the scholarly consumers of the University and the inhabitants of the south western quarter of Oxford (St Ebbe's) in the later medieval and early post-medieval period. The latter will have included inhabitants with a foot in each camp: such as cooks and high ranking college servants who were often owners of cook shops and taverns. These differences give us some insight into consumer choices and the varying levels of prosperity enjoyed within Oxford.

The complete or near complete pots in the collection overall give an excellent introduction to

Fig. 91. Wheel-thrown polychrome tin-glaze earthenware containers from the site of the Forestry Laboratory were found with wine bottles with vintners signs and later college wine bottles, scholar's rubbish perhaps. The illustrated wine bottle has two men playing tennis and the initials 'T. W.' - Thomas Wood architect of the Old Ashmolean also had a tavern and a tennis court on the north side of the city. Mid seventeenth century. Lawrence Collection.

the skill of the potter/craftsman of medieval and later England, and the evolution of ceramic technology. The function of the pottery, the cultural and artistic creativity and the social and economic needs of the consumers and producers can all be explored and the changing tastes must reflect on the political history too. The study of the influences behind the individual ceramic traditions, the shapes of the vessels and their respective decorative elements can be compared and integrated with other artefactual studies.

Above all much of the collection can be placed in its social and economic context within Oxford; most can also be attributed to their likely source of production, and the exploration of these production centres tells us much about the fluctuations of the craft, the craftsmen/artisans and the influences behind their work.

Collecting medieval and later ceramics, by Oxford's amateur archaeologists has left a rich resource that includes much information which is new to the City of Oxford, and some new at national and international level too. This invaluable monument to their vision will continue to draw in students and encourage new interpretations as topographical, architectural and iconographical studies are linked with artefactual and documentary research, and will remain a testimony to the progress of the craftsmen potters and artisans who have shaped the heritage of medieval and later England.

Fig. 92. Hand sketches from the Accessions Book - the finds from Glyn Mills Bank at Carfax include press-moulded industrialised wares; salt-glaze stoneware pepper pot copying a silver shape; creamware mugs; pearlware drinking and serving vessels with some chinese porcelain teawares. This was the first assemblage to be donated by the City Council in 1931. Nineteenth century.

Sites, accession numbers and height of pottery vessels

Reading from left to right unless stated otherwise:-
Fig. 3 Queen St 1959.197; Radcliffe Sq 1915.54; Balliol 1914.631 (Ht. 19.5 cm.; 19 cm.; 26.5 cm.). Fig. 4 Radcliffe Sq 1915.74 inspired by metal vessel, 1915.41; New Bod 1937.861. Front row: High St 1891.7; King Edward St 1872.2431 (Ht. incomplete; 22.5 cm.; 27 cm.; 16.25 cm.; 15 cm.). Fig. 5 Top shelf: King Ed St 1888.1359; tranferred from Bodleian 1887.2007; Glyn Mills 1931.528; no provenance (Ht. 9.3 cm.; 9 cm.; 8.5 cm.; 10.5 cm.). Second shelf: King Ed St 1873.283; Forestry Laboratory 1896.1908 M31; Great College St 1910.455 (Ht. 3.5 cm.; 5.7 cm.; 4.5 cm.). Third shelf: St Giles 1937.653; Burford 1940.12; Rad Sq 1919.7 (Ht. 5.5 cm; 5.5 cm.; 17 cm.). Fourth shelf: London 1966.223; King Ed St 1987.39; Merton Field 1881 (Ht. 3.5 cm.; 3 cm.; 4 cm.). Fig. 6 Old Angel Inn 1876.91; New Bod 1937.512; Radcliffe Camera 1915.60 (Ht. 6 cm.; 11.5 cm.; c. 7.5 cm.). Fig. 7 King Ed St 1873.238; Acotts 1961 no accession no.; King Ed St 1887.3030; 3 Cups Inn 1879.407; Hertford 1909.903 (Ht. 24 cm.; 27.5 cm.; 13 cm.; 15 cm.; 18 cm.). Fig. 8 Top shelf: New College 1896-1908 M46; Christ Church Meadow 1921.224; Unprovenanced 1920.100; 3 Magdalen St 1920.111 (Ht. 11 cm.; 7.5 cm.; 8.25 cm.; 8.5 cm.). Middle shelf: Unprovenanced 1989.24; New Bod 1937.517, 518 c. 1700 AD; Unprovenanced 1920.99; Old Angel Inn 1883.57; Unprovenanced 1986.25; Leopold Arms 1896-1908 M52; George St 1896-1908 M53 (Ht. 17 cm.; 12 cm.; 14.4 cm.; 14.5 cm.; 15 cm.; 12 cm.; 11.5 cm.; incomplete). Fig. 10 New Bod 1937.521; Hertford 1914.633; 109-110 St Aldates 1939.494 (Ht. 28 cm.; 29 cm.; 21.5 cm.). Fig. 13 Bodleian Library, Oxford G A Oxon a65 p85 - no 250. Fig. 14 On shelf: Rad Cam 1915.32, 31 and 34 (Ht. 4 cm.; 4.5 cm.; 8 cm.). On table: 1915.78, 77 and 12 (Ht. 9 cm.; 14 cm.; 14 cm.). In foreground: 1915.51 (Ht. 6.5 cm.). Fig. 15 Bucks County Mus neg. E587; AYBCM:1988.162.1). Fig. 17 Bodleian Library, Oxford John Johnson Coll Trade Cards VI. Fig. 20 Bodleian Library, Oxford Minn Coll neg. 9/59. Fig. 26 18-20 Cornmarket Street 1935.13c, 6, 8, 13d, 13f, 13d, 9 (Ht. incomplete; 6 cm.; 4.5 cm.; 4 cm.; 6.5 cm.; 5 cm.). Fig. 28 Rad Cam 1915.70, 73 (Ht. 29.5 cm.; 31 cm.). Front row: Town Hall 1921.207; New Bod 1937.452 (Ht. 6.5 cm.; 31 cm.). Fig. 29 Rad Cam 1911.259, 1915.71; New Bod 1937.454a and b (Ht. 36 cm.; 31 cm.; 27.5 cm.; 14 c.). Front row: New Bod 1938.1252, 1253; Old Angel Inn 1891.6 (Ht. incomplete; incomplete; 23 cm.). Fig. 31 Bottles: Trinity 1836-1868 p17; Balliol 1921.203 (2). (Ht. 15.5 cm.; 13 cm.; 16 cm.). Rad Cam 1915.15, 16, 79, 80 and 84; Pembroke 1896-1908 M2 (Ht. 11 cm.; 4.8 cm.; 5 cm.; 5.2 cm.; 19 cm.). Fig. 32 Top shelf: George St 1896-1906 M60/2; Fleur-de-Luce 1937.960; University Coll 1883.282; Balliol 1896-1906 M16 (Ht. 34 cm.; 44 cm.; incomplete; 38 cm.). Middle shelf: New Bod 1938.1255; Unprovenanced 1838.107; New Bod 1937.961 (Ht. 26.5 cm.; 24 cm.). Back row: Town Hall 1921.202; Unprovenanced 1896-1908 M4; Halls Brewery St Ebbes 1927.2120 (Ht. 35.5 cm.; 23.5 cm.; 26 cm.). Front row: Town Hall 1921.207; Hertford 1888.106; Rad Cam 1915.47 (Ht. 33 cm.; 21 cm.; 21 cm.). Fig. 34 New Bod 1937.455; Rad Cam 1915.94; New Bod 1938.1258 (Ht. 10.5 cm.; 8.8 cm.; 18 cm.). Fig. 35 Luttrell Psalter, East Anglian, British Library MS. add. 42130, fol. 153. Fig. 36 Top shelf: Rad Cam 1915.40; Broad St 1938.1260; Randolph Hot 1836-1868 p13; New Bod 1938.1262; King Ed St 1874.22 (Ht. incomplete; 19 cm.; 14 cm.; 24 cm.; 25.5 cm.). Second shelf: New Bod 1938.1259; Old Angel Inn 1881.3; University Coll 1892.2617 (Ht. 28 cm.; 23.5 cm.; 30 cm.). Back row: Hertford 1888.116; 18-20 Cornmarket 1935.438, 537; Meadow Building, Christ Church 1887.2548; Campion Hall 1937.862; St Edmund Hall 1935.636; New Bod 1937.443 (Ht. 28 cm.; 23.5 cm.; 30 cm.). Next row: Rad Cam 1915.68; Civet Cat 1935.862; Lincoln Hall 1943.41; London and County Bank 1836-1868 p10 (2); Unprovenanced 1984.1074; University Museum 1896-1908 M17; University Coll 1892.2620; Beaumont St 1940.160 (Ht. 8.5 cm.; 12.5 cm.; 15 cm.; 11cm.; 11 cm.; 16 cm.; 11 cm.; 18 cm.; 10 cm.). Front row: Rad Sq 1915.69; Civet Cat 1896-1908 M177; Fleur-de-Luce 1937.858; Rad Cam 1910.3; Hertford 1887;

Rad Sq 1915.87, 35; Magdalen St 1965.73 (Ht. incomplete; 10 cm.; 3 cm.; 8 cm.; incomplete; 7 cm.; 10 cm.; 8.5 cm.). Fig. 37 Western Art, The Ashmolen Mus neg. no. PA4226. Fig. 38 Rad Cam 1915.57; Unprovenanced 1938.1270; Bod Tunnel 1938 no accession no.; Rad Cam 1915.63 (Ht. 23 cm.; 8.5 cm.; 8.5 cm.; 9 cm.). On table: Hertford 1889.48A; City ditch 1912.1128; Glyn Mills 1931.521; New Coll 1921.206; Oriel 1909.1022 (Ht.19 cm.; 13.5 cm.; 19.5 cm.; 10 cm.; 7.5 cm.). Front: Hertford 1909.904, King Ed St 1889.42; Brill 1887.3035; 3 Cornmarket 1934.63 (Ht. 3 cm.; 3.5 cm.; 8.5 cm.; 4.5 cm.). Fig. 39 Lincoln Hall no accession no.; Blackfriars 1888.1358; Rad Sq 1915.38 (Ht. incomplete; 12 cm.; 5.5 cm.). Fig. 42 New Bod 1938.1204; Turl St 1939.393; Leopold Arms 1896-1908 M45. Fig. 45 Top: Queen St 1937.985; Queen St 1938 no accession no.; Unprovenanced 1948.228; Queen St 1938 no accession no.; Unprovenanced (Ht.16 cm.; 27 cm.; 18 cm.; 12 cm.; 16.5 cm.). Fig. 46 Back row: 1938.403, 380, 379 (Ht. 6 cm.; 21 cm.; 41 cm.). Next row: 402, 396, 382, 381, 384, 395 (Ht. 19.5 cm.; 12 cm.; 14 cm.; 6.9 cm.; 13.5 cm.). Front row: 389, 404, 383, 390, 393, 397, 392. (Ht. 12 cm.; 7 cm.; 5.5 cm.; 5 cm.; 5 cm.; 11 cm.; incomplete; 9 cm.). Fig. 47 Top: New Bod 1937.496. On table: 1937.485, 487, 493, 475, 476, 487 (Ht. incomplete; 6 cm.; 13 cm.; 11 cm.; 16 cm.; 10.5 cm.; 13 cm.). Fig. 48 New Bod 1937.508, 502, 500 and 499 (Ht. 22.5 cm.; 21.5 cm.; 15 cm.; 21 cm.). Fig. 49 Top: Rad Cam 1915.46 (Ht. 19 cm.). Second row: 1915.37, 45, 64; High St 1896-1908 M23; 1915.44, 43; 1910.310; 1915.36 (Ht. 5.4 cm.; 15 cm.; 15 cm.; 7 cm.; 5 cm.; 5.5 cm.; 5.5 cm.; 7.2 cm.; 13 cm.). Fig. 50 On shelf: 1915.30, 81, 29 (Ht. 6 cm.; 1.2 cm.; 6.5 cm.). Foreground: 1911.264 cross joins with 1915.97h; 1915.83 (Ht. 4 cm.; 5 cm.). On table: 1915.19, 20, 9, 22, 21; New Bod 1937.509 (Ht. 20.5 cm.; 16.2 cm.; 9 cm.; 10.5 cm.; 13.2 cm.; 10.5 cm.). Fig. 51 Back row: 1896-1908 M20; 1896-1908 M59; 1896-1908 M58; 1896-1908 M57 (Ht. incomplete; 10 cm.; 14.5 cm.; 14.7 cm.). Front: 1896-1908 M26 (Ht. 5 cm.). On floor: 1907 no accession no.; 1896-1908 M27 (Ht. 18 cm.; 13.5 cm.). Fig. 52 Bodleian Library, Oxford John Johnson - Housing. Fig. 55 Bodleian Library, Oxford Ms. Bodley 264 fol. 170v. Fig. 56 Bodleian Library Ms. Douce 6 fol. 82v. Fig. 57 New Bod 1938.1256; Civet Cat 1971.1225; Trinity 1836.1868 p17; King Edward St 1874.22 (Ht. 36 cm.; 41 cm.; 34 cm.; 25 cm.). Fig. 59 Top: Cornmarket 1896-1908 M3; Town Hall 1894 1896-1908 M173 (Ht. 17 cm.; incomplete). Second row: 39-41 High St 1968.792; All Souls 1921.238; Rad Sq 1972.1025; City Ditch 1873.236; University Coll 1892.2618 (Ht. 17.5 cm.; 17.5 cm.; 17.8 cm.; 23 cm.; 23 cm.). Fig. 68 Bodleian Library, Oxford Minn Coll neg. 12/32. Fig. 69 Oxon. Photographic Archive neg. 1991/ 21/2 Part. Fig. 70 Western Art, The Ashmolean Mus neg. E1313 (ii). Fig. 71 Back row: 1896-1908 M47; 1948.227; 1910.292; 1973.931 (Ht. 26.5 cm.; 22.5 cm.; 20.5 cm.; 23 cm.). Second row: 1896-1908 M48; no accession no. (Ht. 21 cm.; 16 cm.). Front row: 1926.351; 1909.1177; no accession no. (Ht. 9 cm.; 9 cm.; incomplete). Fig. 85 Bodleian Library, Oxford Minn Coll neg. 20/40. Fig. 86 King Edward St Top semi circle: 1874.62, 57, 59 (2). Second semi circle 1896-1908 M36; 1874; 1874.62, 67, 66. Third semi circle: 1874.61, 55, 56, 59. Fourth semi circle: 1874.66 (2), 62, 77. Bottom: 1874.59, 66 (2). Fig. 78 Bodleian Library, Oxford G A Oxon a65, 90, no.266. Fig. 80 Oxon Photographic Archive neg. 2368. Fig. 81 Bodleian Library, Oxford Library Records e.640 no.20. Fig. 82 Bodleian Library, Oxford GA Oxon a65 p49, no. 154. Fig. 84 Bodleian Library, Oxford Minn Coll neg. 64/9. Fig. 85 Bocardo 1921.218, 217; 1896-1908 M52; 1921.220; 1896-1908 M25; 1896-1908 M60 (Ht. 17 cm.; 16.2 cm.; 12.5 cm.; 9 cm.; 7 cm.; 5 cm.). Fig. 87 Bodleian Library, Oxford Minn Coll neg. 3/42. Fig. 88 Bodleian Library, Oxford Manning fol. 24, pl 119. Fig. 90 Bodleian Library, Oxford Manning fol. 24, pl 107. Fig. 91 St John's Forestry Lab 1896-1908 M33; M32, M35, M31 (Ht. 15 cm.; 12.5 cm.; 6.5 cm.; 5.7 cm.). Fig. 92 Glyn Mills 1931.529, 530, 531, 532, 533, 534, 535, 536 (Ht. 11.8 cm.; 12.5 cm.; 14 cm.; 6.5 cm.; 3.8 cm.; 8.5 cm.; 5.5 cm.; 1.4 cm.).

Concise Bibliography

Ashmolean (1868). Ashmolean Museum. 'A List of Donations ...1836 to 1868'. Oxford.

Ashmolean, MS Catalogue. Accessions Index housed in the Department of Antiquities, Ashmolean Museum, Oxford.

Bodleian. The Minute Books of the Oxford Architectural and Historical Society.

Frank Britton, *London Delftware,* (1986).

Ann Brown, *Before Knossos...Arthur Evan's travels in the Balkans and Crete* University of Oxford. Ashmolean Museum. (1993).

R. L. S. Bruce-Mitford, 'The Archaeologist', *Antique Collector,* vol. 1 (1978), 68-9.

Alan Crossley, Chris Day, Janet Cooper, *Shopping in Oxford A Brief History* Oxford Preservation Trust Occ. Paper No. 4 (1983).

Bernard Dragesco, *English Ceramics in French Archives* (1993), privately circulated.

David Gaimster, 'The supply of Rhenish stoneware to London, 1350-1600', *The London Archaeologist* vol. 5, no. 13 (Winter 1987), 339-47.

Dennis Haselgrove and John Murray (eds.) *John Dwight's Fulham Pottery 1672-1978. A Collection of Documentary Sources* (1979).

C. Hibbert and E. Hibbert (eds.) *The Encyclopaedia of Oxford* (1988).

Robin Hildyard, *Browne Muggs* (1985).

David A. Hinton, "Rudely Made Earthen Vessels" of the Twelfth to Fifteenth Centuries A.D.' in D. P. S. Peacock (ed.) *Pottery and Early Commerce* (1977), 221-238.

John G. Hurst, David S. Neal, H. J. E. van Beuningen, *Pottery Produced and Traded in North-West Europe 1350-1650* (1986).

E. M. Jope, 'Saxon Oxford and its region'. in D. B. Harden (ed.) *Dark-Age Britain* (1956), 234-58.

T. E. Lawrence, *Crusader Castles* (1936).

Arthur MacGregor (ed.) *Tradescant's Rarities* (1983).

P. Manning, 'Notes on the Archaeology of Oxford and its Neighbourhood', *Berks. and Bucks. and Oxon. Arch. J.* vol. iv, (1898), 9-28.

P. Manning and E. T. Leeds, 'An Archaeological Survey of Oxfordshire', *Archaeologia* 71, (1921), 227-265.

J. N. L. Myres, *Praeterita* unpublished autobiography.

I. and P. Opie, *The Oxford Dictionnary of Nursery Rhymes* (1951).

R. Plot, *Natural History of Oxford-shire* (1677).

R. Plot, *Natural History of the County of Stafford-shire* (1686).

Rev. H. E. Salter, *Survey of Oxford* W. A. Pantin (ed.) Vol. I and Vol. II, (1960, 1969).

A. V. Simcock, *The Ashmolean Museum and Oxford Science 1683-1983* (1984).

Nancy Stebbing, John Rhodes, Maureen Mellor, The Clay Industries of Oxfordshire *Oxfordshire Potters,* OMSP no. 13 (1980).

D. G. Vaisey and F. Celoria, 'Inventory of George Ecton, 'Potter', of Abingdon, Berks 1696', *Journal of Ceramic History* no. 7, (1974), 13-42.

J. M. Wilson (ed.), *T. E. Lawrence: Letters to E. T. Leeds with commentary by E. T. Leeds* (1988).

See also many articles in *Oxoniensia* and *Medieval Ceramics*

Acknowledgements

I should like to thank Arthur MacGregor for encouraging me to work on the collections and for his sensitive editing of the draft of this text, to Jon Whiteley and Richard Sharp of Western Art for introducing me to some of the archives in the Ashmolean.

To R. L. Bland Archivist, Clifton College, Caroline Dalton Archivist, at New College, John Jones, Dean and Archivist at Balliol for help with past *alumni*; to the archivist at Christ Church for help with Broilliet; to Mike Heaney for broadening my perspective of Manning, to Martin Biddle for a copy of his memorial address of Rupert Bruce-Mitford, to Margaret Bruce-Mitford for further information. To P. R. S. Moorey, Keeper of the Antiquities Department, Ashmolean Museum, for sharing his knowledge; to Rear Admiral Myres for making available his grandfather's papers.

To David Barker, Keeper of Archaeology, City Museum and Art Gallery, Stoke-on-Trent, Julie Edwards, Chester Archaeology, Jacqui Pearce, Museum of London Archaeology Service, Shelagh Vainker, Eastern Art and Timothy Wilson, Western Art, Ashmolean Museum for discussions of non-Oxfordshire wares.

To Brian Durham and John Ashdown who patiently unravelled any misconceptions I may have entertained about Oxford's topography.

The inspirational photographs were taken by Jane Inskipp and Anne Holly; Nick Griffiths drew the map and illustrations, to them all I am deeply indebted.

The majority of the photographs are reproduced by courtesy of the Visitors of the Ashmolean Museum, with the exception of Fig. 15 courtesy of Buckinghamshire County Museum; Fig. 18 courtesy of The Victorian and Albert Museum; Figs. 20, 52, 55, 56, 68, 78, 81, 82, 84, 85, 87, 88, 90 courtesy of the Bodleian Library; Fig. 25 courtesy of the Trustees of the British Museum; Fig. 35 courtesy of the British Library; Fig. 53 courtesy of Oxfordshire Museum Services; Figs. 60 and 61 courtesy of the Museum of the History of Science, Oxford; Figs. 69, 80 courtesy of Oxfordshire Photographic Archive and Fig. 74 courtesy of the Courtauld Institute of Art.